A Portrait of the Student as a Young Wolf:

If a dog made up an IQ test, most people would probably flunk it.

Motivating Undergraduates

Other Books by
Darby Lewes

Dream Revisionaries:
Gender and Genre in Women's Utopian
Fiction, 1870-1920

Nudes from Nowhere:
Utopian Sexual Landscapes

A Brighter Morn:
The Shelley Circle's Utopian Project

Auto-poetica: Representations of the
Creative Process in Nineteenth-century
British and American Fiction

Double Visions: Eighteenth- and
Nineteenth-century Literary Palimpsests

A Portrait of the Student as a Young Wolf:

Motivating Undergraduates

"Every teacher should have been an animal trainer at some time in his career, because when the animal doesn't do the trick, you don't blame the animal!"

Darby
Lewes
and
Bobby
Stiklus

Illustrations by Jennifer Gray

Printing History

1. Softcover Bowling Green State University Composition Retreat Edition 1, July, 2003.
2. Edition 2, Perfect Binding, September, 2003
3. Edition 3, Perfect Binding, September 2007

For Tom Mitchell

"A teacher affects eternity; he can never tell
where his influence stops."
—Henry B. Adams

"Good teachers are usually a little crazy."
— Andy Rooney

Acknowledgements

How on earth can I ever sufficiently thank

John Piper, Janet Hurlburt , and Charles Mahler
of Lycoming College?

or Milt Cox, Melody Barton , Laurie Richlin,
Gregg Wentzell, Gabriele Bauer
and the rest of the wonderful folks at the
Lilly Teaching Excellence conferences?

or Douglas Eder, Todd Zakrajsek, Alan Kalish, Kathryn Plank,, Luz
Mangurian, Ron Berk, Pete Beidler, Gwynedd T. Dog UD NA NAJ,
and the rest of the folks who did not think the idea for this book
was totally insane?

or the kid?

or my dear, dear friend and Border Colleague,
Sheepy Hollow's Folly, UDX, OA, OAJ
whose shoes will never be filled by another?

No way can I thank you folks enough. But I love you all.
Especially the kid.

Table of Contents

Preface

> "Wow. This class makes a lot more sense when I read the book."

—Student comment
English 106, 1997

W hen I was a graduate student (back during the Punic Wars), I used to dream of the day I would finally be a full-time teacher, and envision what my classes would be like. It was a lovely picture. Something a lot like the one on the right.

I could see it clearly. I would be standing in front of a group of bright, eager young people, giving them the benefits of my wisdom as they waved their hands enthusiastically and took notes feverishly. They would laugh uproariously at the hilarious jokes I would sprinkle into my lectures. They would follow me into the hall after class, and clump around my office, waiting to discuss books they'd read, and ideas they'd generated. It would be heaven.

When I finally did stand in front of my first real class, however, I found the situation to be considerably different than the one I had anticipated. It was something a lot like this:

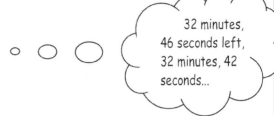

32 minutes, 46 seconds left, 32 minutes, 42 seconds...

The joyous faces of my grad-school dreams were nowhere in evidence. The students who faced me were bored, stressed, and grade-obsessed. The papers they wrote were peppered with misspellings and typos, and were dull beyond belief: obviously written without care, without pride, without hope. The subtext was clear. The students did not like my subject, did not like my class, and weren't particularly thrilled about me. Some stared dully into space, accepting the class as a vague punishment for unknown sins; some carved obscenities into their desks; some slept.

Of course I found this situation depressing — wouldn't any sage on the stage feel the same way? Was this how I would spend the next thirty or forty years of my life? Yet the situation was also uniquely frustrating to me, however. Here's why.

For nearly a half century (I began when Eisenhower was in office), I had been successfully training and showing purebred dogs, working with what I considered to be my canine colleagues as part of a team. My frustration with my students was a reaction to the fact that they weren't contributing anything to our "team." Oh, they would do what I told them ("open your text to page 135," "take out a sheet of paper"), and they would jam my lectures into their short-term memory and parrot them back to me on exams and in papers. But that was it. I was unable to transfer the excitement I felt about my subject to my students; they were taking nothing away from the class that would belong to them—that would somehow become an important part of their life experiences. I was furious with them, but I was far more furious with myself: I could get a dog to work with me as a partner and equal, but I couldn't motivate a human being—and a bright human being, a human being who had made it through high school and into college—to do the same thing.

> "I can't give you a brain, but I can give you a diploma."
>
> —Wizard of Oz

Admittedly, I wasn't totally incompetent. I could teach them to do the human equivalent of jumping over a stick (or, to use more academic terms, through a hoop). My problem was that I wanted to teach far more than just a specific behavior. I wanted to teach students to enjoy that behavior, and to apply it to other situations. I was trying to teach them how to become equal partners in the teacher-student team, and to do so to such an extent that their preconceived notions of teacher and student blurred into a single, absolutely galvanizing learning experience: Hell, I wanted them to enjoy learning as much as a dog did. So I went back and re-examined how I had developed as an animal trainer, in the hope that I could develop in the same way as a teacher.

I had seen dog training undergo a variety of fashions during five decades.

During the 1950s and 1960s, it was pretty much a military type of affair, developed from what people had learned about training dogs during World War II and Korea. The trainer/drill sergeant would jerk the dog around on a choke chain and reward the animal with a pat or praise when it did what it was told. The dogs eventually became fairly reliable and precise—although not particularly enthusiastic, unless they got to attack someone (now, that was FUN!!!). Those dogs who could not be motivated with a pat on the head—either because they were too stupid to get the idea or too intelligent to settle for someone else's agenda—washed out. In academia, we call this form of teaching "lecturing."

Look closely at the faces of these two students, canine and human. Do you see the similarity of attitude toward this form of education? All that's missing on the face of the young blonde woman is the muzzle.

In the late seventies, a sort of feel-good, flower-child philosophy bloomed, and a new style of training emerged, which was immediately dismissed as "cookie pushing" by the old-timers. The idea was to reward the dog for everything—a training session was one long happy cheese-liver-chicken smorgasbord. The advantages were obvious: instead of a bored dog working because he had to (and with lowered tail and head that made his point of view embarrassingly clear), an enthusiastic dog now pranced around the training ring with head held high, tail wagging, thrilled with the chance to earn some lovely snacks. All dogs were wonderful; all dogs were happy. Academics call this "grade inflation."

You want it? *You* pick it up.

There are drawbacks to cookie pushing and grade inflation, of course: no cookie, no effort. Animals, who would work eagerly at home where it was worth their while to do so, took very little time to figure out that the handler could not carry treats into the dog show ring. No food, no interest. Students faced with un-inflated teaching shut down almost as quickly. In each case, the student was working for the short-term reward of a cookie or grade—not even considering, let alone encountering, the reward of learning.

In the 1980s, however, the dog-training cookie-pushers rediscovered B. F. Skinner, and began to use his innovative behavior modification techniques on their dogs. Training became more and more sophisticated, and animal motivation was at its center. The dog and handler became a team, with each of them contributing appropriately to the total effort. Cookies were gradually phased out; delayed, or "conditioned" reinforcers (I'll discuss these terms in more detail later) were gradually phased in. And it worked.

The dogs—both the "smart" dogs and the "dumb" dogs, even breeds such as Afghans, which had been bred for centuries to resist working in teams in favor of independent hunting—began to work for a variety of reasons. Food and other tangible rewards were still a substantial part of their motivation, but elements such as teamwork, play, and the fun of learning were now also important.

Academics had a number of names for this sort of thing, mostly unprintable. "Brainwashing" was among the kindest.

After I considered the various kinds of animal training I had encountered over the years, the true nature of the problem—and the solution—suddenly hit me. College education and dog training had paralleled one another for a long time, and enjoyed similar successes and failures. But dog training had—bravely or not—somehow gone where the majority of educators (including me) had either feared to tread or just never thought of going.

Lecturing had been the primary teaching method when I was in college and graduate school. My teachers—and I—had been using the human version of the old military jerk-and-praise model: I wasn't motivating my students at all; I was treating them like sponges who would absorb my wisdom and wring it back out on command. If they couldn't do that at least 60% of the time (and get a passing "D"), they washed out of the program. What I needed to do was rethink my teaching methods in the same way I had rethought my training methods.

Although my dog-training friends thought I was on the right track, I couldn't really discuss this epiphany with any of my academic colleagues—they would have been horrified by the notion of manipulating students with behavior modification. And yet, I realized that I was already manipulating my students: I was training them to sit submissively through a lecture and not interrupt (politeness, respect) how to write down whatever I said (or whatever they thought I had said), and how to deal with boredom, spoon-fed minute by agonizing minute, one hour at a time.

There was also the problem of what my colleagues might think of my treating students "like dogs." Not a problem for me, actually: I love and respect my dogs tremendously; they are generous and caring friends who teach me as much as I teach them. But people who have never had a deep relationship with a dog might find my metaphor rather off-putting.[1]

Yet dogs and humans have a great deal in common. We both began as distance runners, and learned to adapt to a wide variety of situations and climates: hence, there's a certain amount of flexibility hard-wired into our natures. We're both omnivores, open to new ideas in food and life. We both adhere to a hierarchical social structure, in which intangibles such as status are tremendously important. We're group hunters, implementing teamwork and mutual dependence. We are both highly fluent in body language — a raised eyebrow or tail can speak multitudes.

And, perhaps most important, we are both readily motivated. We want rewards, both tangible and intangible. We seek validation, assurances that we're doing a good job. We fear discomfort: pain, confusion, and vulnerability; and seek to avoid it whenever — and by any means — possible.

This capacity for motivation is of course the basis of this book, and raises a question.

Why should students need to be motivated? Shouldn't education be its own reward? After all, my idea of a perfect evening is sitting down with a glass of wine and some Dickens — sherry if I'm reading Jane Austen. The next morning, I'll go to "work" and discuss my reading with a group of young people who presumably spent the previous evening in a similarly delightful manner.

---

[1] Indeed, the original title of this volume was *A Portrait of the Student as a Young Dog*, which I intended to be a blended *homage à* James Joyce's *Portrait of the Artist as a Young Man* and Dylan Thomas' *Portrait of the Artist as a Young Dog*. So many of my academic colleagues were horrified by the student/canine association, however, that I changed the title. Interestingly, no one had any problems whatsoever with the metaphor of student as wolf.

Since everyone's having such a delightful time, why on earth would people engaged in the study of (fill in your discipline) need anything as grossly manipulative as "motivation"? If I'm a good teacher, my enthusiasm will infect my students, won't it? And if these students didn't enjoy the study of (discipline) in the first place, they wouldn't be in my class, would they?

Well, they do. And it won't. And they are—because they must be. It's a paradox that one old fellow has been trying to explain for centuries.

Flash! Extra! Plato was right!

(Well, actually, *Socrates* was right, but he never published, so…)

I n Book Seven of The Republic, Plato presents a schematic for education in his ideal society. Interestingly, he schedules his curriculum according to age, rather than ability. And he makes some very provocative assertions.

Young people, he assures us, have absolutely no business studying

Platonic Puppy

philosophy. They are too immature to understand its nature, and will tend to misuse what they learn, using ideas merely "to contradict … like puppies,[2] enjoying pulling and tearing with argument at those who happen to be near" (539b). Indeed, in this best of all possible worlds, young people do not actually "study" anything. They receive instruction in morality (by listening to stories, a favorite youthful pastime), and mathematics (by playing number games), but "the instruction must not be given the aspect of a compulsion to learn" (536d).

Older youths — the rough equivalent of our college students — devote their primary attention to subjects befitting their age and abilities: music, gymnastics (which produce "weariness and sleep," the "enemies of studies"), and war — although it's not *real* war for

---

[2] I guess my human/dog analogy wasn't *totally* original.

them: they are "led to war on horseback as spectators; and, if it's safe anywhere, they must be led up near and taste blood, like puppies" (537a). They should also bear children at this age, since they are at the height of their sexual potential.

Our *Republic*-an teenagers, then, will spend their days (and nights) in a perpetual round of music, dance, pretend warfare, and sex. If we were to translate their experience into modern terms, we might see kids who listen to a lot of music, dance, play sports and video games (and watch a lot of action movies), and have sex. In short, teenagers who do exactly what most college students would do if left to their own devices.

People are not really equipped to study "philosophy" (a deeply intellectual process which, in today's terms, would translate into most college studies) until they hit thirty, Plato argues. Imagine that. What would your classroom be like if it were filled exclusively with thirty-year-olds?

Think of it for a moment—a room full of continuing education students. If they're anything like the continuing education students I've run into, they're motivated beyond belief, doing not only the assigned reading but bringing in ancillary materials they discovered on their own, contributing eagerly to intelligent, thoughtful class discussions, and sighing with disappointment when the class is over.

I should point out that I know whereof I speak, here. I graduated from high school in the upper four-fifths of my class, thoroughly convinced that education was an invidious plot perpetuated by the envious old upon the vigorous young. I then unwittingly followed Platonic guidelines: I enjoyed a fifteen-year career as a musician, and reared two children. When, in my early thirties, I started feeling a bit long in the tooth for enthusiastic renditions of "Proud Mary," I began my undergraduate career.

School had certainly changed, I thought, not realizing that it was I who had done the changing. And, although I at first despaired of "keeping up" with the bright young minds around me, so freshly graduated from high school, I found that, as the saying goes, youth and vigor were no match for old age and cunning. And certainly no match for my newly acquired hyper-motivation.

Ha. Told you so. But did you listen? Noooo....

To this day, I am convinced that were Plato's theories on education put into practice — if college classes were indeed filled with mature adults — writing a book about student motivation would be about as silly and pointless as writing one on how to get teenagers to play more video games.

But as teachers, we must work with what we have: traditional — *i.e.*, late adolescent students, neck-deep in hormones and generally far more concerned with the outcome of Saturday's football game or Heather's new significant other than the quadratic equation you just wrote on the board.

We would seem to be bucking an almost insurmountable current—how can the Teutonic wonders of German noun declensions or the lurking menace of a split infinitive ever compete with the excitement of sex, rock and roll, and *Pirates of the Caribbean*?

Don't despair. It's the same problem I face every time I try to persuade a dog that coming when I call is of more inherent value than chasing a rabbit.

Yet dogs can be motivated to abandon the hunt and return to their human pack member, and traditional students can be taught to be part of the student-teacher team. Indeed, after a while, notions of who is teaching whom can become wonderfully hazy. It's a terrific experience to work with a student—human or dog—who has blurred work and play into a single, satisfying activity. Imagine: what would teaching be like if your students—canine or human—could come to think of education as an exciting and valuable endeavor, right up there with chasing a rabbit or playing a video game?

That is exactly the type of classroom atmosphere I hope this book will help you create.

A Portrait of the Student as a Young Wolf:

"Wisdom begins in wonder."
—Socrates

I wonder what's for dinner.

Motivating Undergraduates

Part I
Reinforcing Students

"Mostly I really like teachers who aren't your enemy — I hate the ones who are always looking for ways to flunk you. The best kind of teacher really wants you to learn and is really glad when you do."

— Anonymous student comment,
English 106 class evaluation, 1994

"She left her signature on us, the literature of the teacher who writes on minds. I have had many teachers who told me soon-forgotten facts but only three who created in me a new thing, a new attitude, a new hunger. I suppose that to a large extent I am the unsigned manuscript of that high school teacher. What deathless power lies in the hand of such a person."
— John Steinbeck

1
"Natural" Aversion

"Natural" Aversion,
the Distribution Course,
and Pure Positive Reinforcement

> "Potry [sic] sucks."

—Anonymous student,
in-class written comment, English 215, 1994

Every teacher, regardless of discipline, must teach it at some point in his or her career: the distribution course, populated almost entirely by non-majors who are there simply because they must be. These students often assert that they "hate" the subject matter because it's inherently stupid, boring, and pointless. Actually however, it's fear, rather than distaste, that generates their negative opinion. They're positive that they're not "good" at the topic and are terrified that they will wind up with not only a rotten grade, but (perhaps even more frightening) public awareness of what they perceive as intellectual inadequacy. And, since no one wants to look like an idiot in front of one's peers, defense mechanisms kick in: studied indifference and/or sullen hostility abound. Students may also attempt to deal with their fears by giving the courses alternate, less terrifying titles: Art Appreciation 101 is re-christened "Art in the Dark" by iconophobes; Geology 101 becomes "Rocks for Jocks," and Math 100, "Math for Morons."

> "The most extraordinary thing about a really good teacher is that he or she transcends accepted educational methods."
>
> — Margaret Mead

The distaste is what dog trainers call "natural" aversion. I put "natural" in quotes because it may not be natural at all, but rather a product of social conditioning. A dog who was severely punished for chewing shoes as a puppy might have a "natural" aversion to carrying objects made of leather; a female student who heard as a child that girls were not good at numbers might have a similar "natural" aversion to mathematics.

Such aversion among students is fairly common, and many teachers dismiss it as nothing more than an inescapable hazard of the profession. Yet it is far more than that. "Natural" aversion is an insurmountable wall between the teacher and the student. Speaking as a teacher, trainer, and long-standing functional innumerate, I am certain that *it is virtually impossible to teach a subject with any degree of lasting understanding until the student's natural aversion has been overcome.* The instructor must first overcome student certainty that they are doomed to failure and/or humiliation.

Right. That's *all* you have to do?

I'll admit that this important process of reconditioning is not an easy task. It can require considerable time, energy, and creativity. Here's an example. I live and work with a Border Collie named Folly (she's the furry one on the cover of this book) who had a "natural" aversion to metal. I have no idea why; perhaps she simply hated the taste of it. As far as I know, she was never beaten with a tablespoon.

> "You can lead a boy to college, but you cannot make him think."
>
> — Elbert Hubbard

> "Do you lead your students to the water and make them drink or do you try harder to make them thirsty?"
>
> — Carter G. Woodson

In advanced obedience, however, a dog must retrieve a metal dumbbell as part of the scent discrimination exercise. I could have forced her to carry the metal despite her aversion, and she would have done it just to shut me up. But she would have always hated the exercise — and that wouldn't have been much fun for either of us. And she would have memorized the exercise by rote, not learning anything about it except what she absolutely *had* to. Retrieving a metal article would not have taught her to retrieve a spoon, for example. I'd have to teach that as a separate exercise. If anything unusual happened during the scent retrieve (if a bee stung her on the nose when she went out to get the article), she would have shut down. A student who works out of fear of punishment tends to panic when suddenly called upon to think outside the box: *i.e.*, to be an active participant in her own education.

Here's what I did to overcome the problem.

Folly, like most dogs, loves nothing so much as a ride in the car. So I put a small leather "Coach" tab on my key chain (she has no aversion to leather, and I have no aversion to Coach's products), and had her carry my keys for me. She soon learned that carrying the keys meant a ride, and would grab them from the table whenever I got ready to go somewhere. In her eagerness, she sometimes forgot to grab the leather tab; eventually, I removed it. Keys—and the taste of metal—became associated with something wonderful, and to this day she will retrieve metal articles with alacrity.

> "A teacher who can arouse a feeling for one single good poem accomplishes more than he who fills our memory with rows and rows of natural objects, classified with name and form."
>
> — Johann Wolfgang von Goethe

Indeed, when a bee *did* sting her on the nose as she went out to retrieve the metal article at a summer show, she was unfazed—completed the exercise, and took a ribbon. A student who works for the joy of working has no difficulty thinking outside the box: she is an active and enthusiastic participant in her own education.

But how on earth can one achieve the same positive results with students who have *already* been badly stung in math, or English, or science, and now loathe the subject? Well, first by realizing the cause of their "natural" aversion: Folly's was probably a matter of taste; as I noted above, student aversion is most often a matter of fear. As Alfie Kohn points out, "The truth is that kids are *constantly* fearful of getting things wrong, which is why they do as little as they can get away with" (159, original emphasis). (For those readers who think it odd—even heretical—to cite Alfie Kohn on a book half-filled with behaviorism, please read section 4.2 below.) People, especially adolescents, are afraid of looking stupid. They like to engage in things they are "good" at. They like to feel smart. And they like tangible proof—trophies, ribbons, awards, high grades—of their skill.

One of the most effective ways to overcome "natural" aversion in humans (or dogs) is to completely eliminate their fears through pure positive reinforcement (often called "PPR" by behaviorists). This is the "cookie-pushing" method of dog training. Although PPR is highly *in*effective in the long haul, and will rarely be of much use in generating long-term learning or self-motivation, it is nonetheless the easiest, and perhaps the only consistent way that students' fear of a given subject—their "natural" aversion—can be *reliably* overcome.

Here's how I use PPR in the dreaded "English 215: Introduction to Literary Interpretation" (dubbed "Lit for Linebackers" by students). English 215 is described in the catalog as "Practice in the methods of close reading and formal analysis; identification of primary elements and structures of literary presentation." Students who are genuinely interested in the discipline of English Literature tend to take the more grueling 200-level survey courses, so my 215 class is invariably filled with non-majors who consider it to be the least detestable (*i.e.*, the "easiest") of the required humanities offerings. The class is thus at once simultaneously unpopular and packed to the rafters.

Poetry, with its intense and condensed language, is the medium in which those "primary elements and structures" so highly touted in the catalog can be most readily isolated, and is consequently the most useful in an introductory class. When, fresh out of grad school, I taught the Intro to Lit class for the first time, I asked students to jot down (anonymously) their (presumably positive) initial response to the word "poetry."

That evening, I settled in with a glass of wine, ready to savor my results. The first response sheet was disheartening, to say the least. "Poetry is dumb and boring."

Okay. Well, things had to get better. I looked at the second response.

"Potry [sic] sucks."

Poetryawn…

Oh, dear. With sinking heart, I turned to the third response, and then the fourth. They grew worse and worse, until finally I reached what had to be the absolute nadir: "Poetry is written by a bunch of queers for another bunch of queers to read."

I could go no farther. And I switched to scotch.

Clearly, I *was not* dealing with like minds—well, maybe they were of a kind, but not my kind—and I was far too inexperienced a teacher to realize that what I *was* dealing with was natural aversion. My initial attempts to engage students were a series of fiascoes.

Convinced that their distaste was based on their lack of experience with really "good" poetry, I inundated them with the best of the best: Milton's sonnet on his blindness, Gray's "Country Churchyard" elegy, Shakespeare's "fortune and men's eyes" sonnet. Student resistance was almost palpable.

Next, smugly convinced that it was *language* that was at the root of their distaste, I tried using ultra "cool" poetry—the work of Bob Dylan and Jim Morrison, for example. This was met with rolled eyes and the surreptitious flashing of peace signs.

"Lay Lady lay…
Good girl!"
♫

Finally, sure that the problem was generational, I introduced examples of "their" poetry: hip-hop and rap. But while I learned a great deal about rap imagery ("I ain't gone send him on his way/Put him up in that big caddy," for example, means that the narrator has no immediate plans to murder his associate), I discovered the students learned little or nothing about "primary elements and structures of literary presentation."

Back at square one, I began again, this time establishing a specific minimum set of goals for the first class:

1. Make the reading of a poem a positive experience.

Okay, perhaps that was going too far. But I had at least finally managed to identify part of the *real* problem: poetry was a foreign language that made my negatively averse students feel like lost wayfarers, adrift in an alien world inhabited by sneaky synedoches and treacherous tropes. Even if I couldn't make the students actually *like* the material, perhaps I could show them that there was nothing inherently scary about it. I amended my first goal to

1. Make the reading of a poem a *non-negative* experience. That seemed like a good start. But even such a relatively modest goal had its pitfalls: in order to move them from negative to neutral, I would have to demystify the text, somehow make it less intimidating. In a logical, down-to-earth way, I would have to…

2. Teach students the rudiments of close reading. Then, assuming I could manage that feat, I'd still have to establish some sort of a goal, a finish line that they could cross successfully. These kids weren't going to work for some touchy-feely nonsense about how literature enriched the mind. I'd have to make the poem a game that they could win, a puzzle that they could solve. Aha! I would…

> "Education is not the filling of a pail, but the lighting of a fire."
>
> — W. B. Yeats

3. Teach them to isolate a theme. Then, when (if?) they solved that puzzle, I'd come up with a slightly tougher (not *too* much tougher) brainteaser; *got it!* Using a similar piece of verse, I would…

4. Teach them to compare two works and recognize thematic similarities. And, since this class would probably afford them the only exposure to "serious" literature that many of them would ever receive, I would figure out some way to…

5. Use a canonical text. Yeah, that last one was tough. Milton was out for the time being. Ditto Shakespeare, Eliot, Keats, Sidney, Spenser, Donne, Tennyson, Yeats …. But I had a secret weapon in my literary arsenal: Robert Browning's "Porphyria's Lover."

If you're not familiar with it, "Porphyria's Lover" is a creepy little poem about a sociopath who strangles his girlfriend. (It's in *Appendix 1*, just in case you'd like to look at it before reading further). Although written in semi-elevated language, it tells a story of sex and violence with which virtually any 20th-century adolescent can identify.

Was I pandering to my students' baser elements by making such a sensationalistic, even titillating selection? Perhaps. But I remembered Plato's assertion that young people dealt more easily with sex and violence than with philosophy. And the poem wasn't *National Enquirer* material, after all; it had a number of very important messages to impart. And anyway, I was nowhere near trying to elevate them at that point; I was just trying to overcome negative aversion. I hope the following digression will explain my choice.

"If I ran a school, I'd give the average grade to the ones who gave me all the right answers, for being good parrots. I'd give the top grades to those who made a lot of mistakes and told me about them, and then told me what they learned from them."

--R. Buckminster Fuller

Digression

When working toward eliminating natural aversion, teachers should aim toward the interests of their audience, not themselves. Reinforcers are relative; what you might perceive as a reward (reading a book, for example) might be a punishment for someone else. Gifted science teachers do not overcome natural aversion to physics by employing cutting-edge and probably esoteric topics that interest *them*; instead they use shaving cream and balloons to demonstrate its principles. Or they overcome natural aversion to chemistry by blowing something up. They juggle. They tap dance. One incredibly brilliant Chemistry professor at my school has worked out a presentation (which takes seven hours to set up) wherein he plays the "1812 Overture" on a CD and the preset chemical reactions go off precisely in time to serve the function of cannon. Yes, it might seem silly. Yes, you might seem to be "pandering" to your audience. But I will restate my belief that *it is impossible to teach a subject with any degree of lasting understanding until natural aversion has been overcome.* I suppose my motto here would be "Whatever it takes." "Pandering"—if that's indeed what engaging student attention is— is a small price to pay to open up the wonders of your discipline to a young mind who would otherwise be too intimidated to engage it.

I remember exactly one thing about high school chemistry, which I failed spectacularly—twice. One day we had a substitute teacher; to warm us up, he put the diagram below on the board and asked us what it was:

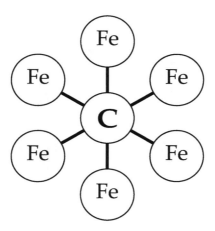

Although I was the Official Chemistry Dim Bulb, I was the only person who answered the question correctly: as you can clearly see, it's a Ferrous Wheel. For one glorious moment, I felt really smart — indeed, that was the only time I ever felt smart in Chemistry. To this day, I still remember that Fe = iron. And to this day, the above diagram is the *only* warm and fuzzy memory I have of Chemistry. In fact, it's the only memory of Chemistry I have at all. What does that tell you?

And now, back to our regularly scheduled text:

So, "Porphyria's Lover." I knew what text we were going to work with. But *how* would we work with it? Group work was out; the hostility levels were far too high. Put the students together and they'd start working on ways to blow up my car. A lecture would let them tune out and drift away; they were already *way* too good at that. I struck upon a method that was at once safe, yet highly confrontational: I would read the poem aloud, then trigger their own innate prey drive (see below) by moving directly into the seating area—*their* area—and posing direct but open-ended questions ***that would be impossible to get "wrong."*** I still use the process today—every day, in one form or another, and in every class, with any student who is floundering. It's called Pure Positive Reinforcement.

Here's how it works.

> "Good teaching is one-fourth preparation and three-fourths theater."
>
> — Gail Godwin

The first question I present to my hostile group is vague, and not really meant to be answered. Thus, it is posed to the class as a whole: "Tell me about the narrator." No response. But that's OK. I've made my point. I'm not going to roll my eyes and mutter about student apathy. No one has answered, but the world hasn't ended.

Then I move to an individual student and ask a direct question, one that no student has ever gotten "wrong": "would you fix him up on a date with your sister—assuming, that is, that you *like* your sister?"

The invariably heartfelt response: "No way!"

I back away from the individual, but stay on the fringes of his space, scanning the class. Then I ask innocently: "Why not?" I'm flooded with answers.

Bingo. By answering the second and third questions, the students have changed their world in two small ways. First, the kids have — some of them for the first time in their lives — volunteered to open a discussion in an English class, *and nothing horrible happened.* They feel daring and brave. Second, they made a critical judgment about the narrator — "'Cause he's a freaking psycho, man!" — and it was spot-on correct. The tiniest seeds of confidence have been sown.

> "What is education but a process by which a person begins to learn how to learn?"
>
> — Peter Ustinov

At this point — very carefully, very slowly — I begin to engage them in close reading, in the guise of a game. I ask them at what point in the poem they first realized that the narrator was (ahem) rationally challenged. They'll point to the strangulation scene (line 41 in a 60 line poem) and I'll say, "Very good. But *I* (ha-*ha*!) figured it out earlier!"

Silence. Long pause. "Well," one brave heart points out, rising to the implied challenge, "I thought it was kind of weird where she talked to him and he wouldn't talk back to *her*" (line 15 — we're making progress). "Excellent!" I reply. "But I figured it out even before that!"

They work backward again. "Well," points out another student, "it's like *really* strange that he's just like sitting in this cabin with no fire or light or anything..." (line 6). "Yup," I reply, "You're absolutely right; it sure is. But..." (they groan here) "I can take it back even further."

They know they have to be close, now. After all, they're down to six lines (and are doing really close reading for the first time in their lives).

"Wind can't be sullen," they finally realize (line 2). "No," I agree, "it can't." By George, they've gotten it. Through a reversive process, they've managed to determine that if wind cannot be sullen, the sullenness must be coming from the speaker. And, just as importantly, they now realize that Browning has inserted *several* careful hints about the narrator's state of mind from the very beginning of the poem. [3]

Then we move to the character of Porphyria.

And that's how we get through the poem. I'm in their spaces and in their faces — there is no escape — but there are also *absolutely no negatives*. Starting with open questions to feed discussion, I then frame more focused questions in such a way that the student is almost locked into a correct response. Okay, sometimes a student *still* doesn't come up with the answer I'm looking for. Sometimes, despite my best efforts at channeling them toward a correct answer, students still manage to come up with ideas that are flat-out *wrong*. Then it's my turn to show what a real teacher's made of.

As far as I'm concerned, my finest hour as an educator occurred when a very tentative student asked me what William Shakespeare (1564-1616) thought of Dr. Samuel Johnson's (1709-1784) critique of his work. The rest of the class looked at me warily — would I stomp

---

[3] In fact, Browning actually raises questions about the narrator's sanity even earlier — in the title. Porphyria, after all, is the hereditary disease that drove George III of England to insanity. The "old, mad, blind, despised, and dying king" (Shelley, "England in 1819") was often seen engaging in intense foreign policy discussions with trees.

this poor anachronistic fool? Nope. Instead, I turned his remark into a "good" question:

"Wow! What a terrific idea! What *would* Shakespeare have thought of Doctor Johnson's critique? How *did* the world view of a seventeenth-century English Renaissance playwright differ from that of an eighteenth-century Enlightenment author?"

Not only did the poor student escape humiliation—indeed, by the time I was through, he seemed rather pleased with himself for instigating such cutting edge debate, but the remainder of the class was assured that the classroom was a safe place to try out new ideas and to take chances. As Alfie Kohn points out, a student's

> …image of himself as smart or competent is endangered by the risk of failing to meet a certain standard of performance. The attempt to protect that image usually comes at the expense of one's attempt to try one's best, which can seem risky. If you don't try, you can't fail (156).

Or, I would argue, if you *can't* fail as long as you're trying, you can't fail. When everyone in the class, despite their level of understanding, realizes that no one who's making any sort of attempt to come to grips with the material is going to be singled out for humiliation, tension leaves the room like a blast of stagnant air.

I'm shameless about rewarding thoughtful—or even conscious—responses. From the first day of class, I'll slam down a "handsome silver trophy" (a quarter) on the desk of a student who's making any sort of effort at all.

> "Why teach? Why did Prometheus steal fire only to turn around and give it away? There is an inherent generosity in the human spirit-one of its faces is the face of the teacher."
>
> —Michael Crichton

Mini-Digression

Q uarters. Ah, yes. I experimented with a variety of tangible rewards — miniature candy bars, for example — and found the results mixed at best. Not everyone likes chocolate (particularly if the class is held at eight in the morning); many students are on diets. Some are allergic to chocolate. And, although this might be hard for you to believe, some people actually *do not like* chocolate (!).

When I brought in little toys and games that my husband brought back from computer trade shows, the students seemed to feel that they were getting second-hand junk palmed off on them. Trophies and medals were considered hokey and juvenile bribes. Stickers? I won't even go there. Quarters, on the other hand, are the lifeblood of student existence. They feed washers and dryers, soft drink and candy machines, photocopiers and video games. What else is there in college?

One thing, though. Don't make the mistake that I did — tossing quarters to the students. I used to do so, until one student complained on a student evaluation, "I felt like a trained seal." Now I haul my not inconsiderable butt up to the individual and place the coin directly on his desk or in her hand. Oh — and if a student should ever indicate even the vaguest discomfort about accepting quarters, be sure find him an alternate reward.[4]

---

[4] Note: Quarters can also come in handy if a few pushy Alpha students dominate class discussion. Point out that in order to share the wealth, quarter-ed students must pipe down for ten minutes after they earn each coin. Alphas realize that all (even lower status) pack members must be fed and won't quibble.

A Micro-Digression on a Mini-Digression

An important aside here—if the tangible rewards a teacher/trainer gives out to reduce "natural" aversion do not have the desired effect (*i.e.*, if students do not actively perceive them as rewards) the teacher should *not* bother wasting time and energy griping about ungrateful students, but set about to find a better reinforcer. Let's say, for example, that Folly the metal-hater didn't particularly care about rides in the car. I would have found something she did care about: peanut butter on a metal spoon, perhaps, until she associated the reward with the metal. If my aversive students should ever not want quarters (this has never happened), I'd reward them with one of Folly's Stupid Dog Tricks, or getting out of class a few minutes early. If they didn't like that, I'd keep experimenting.

Think about it. Folly will do almost anything for a piece of raw liver. Yum, yum.
How about you?

You'd probably do almost anything for a million dollars.

But would Folly?

Meanwhile, back at the book...

Quarters are great, but the biggest Pure Positive Reinforcement (PPR) is that students start to feel smart, a self-reinforcer if there ever was one. They'll also begin competing for the reward not because they really need the quarter, but because the self-reinforcer has transmogrified a mere two-bit piece into a tangible emblem of intellectual success. And success in the very subject they once feared. (At graduation a few years ago, I discovered that one fullback (who wound up minoring in English) had carried the first "handsome silver trophy" (quarter) I awarded him for *three years* as a lucky piece.)

After we've covered the entire poem, I give a short, manageable, in-class assignment (again, one that is virtually impossible to get wrong).

"Pick one word that is essential to the poem (and have a backup or two in case someone else takes 'your' word)."

Browning's a good enough poet to have chosen every word carefully. And by now, twenty solid minutes of PPR has convinced the students that they have a decent shot at a "right" answer and won't be ridiculed for a "wrong" one.[5] I carefully write "their" word on the board: if the student is weak—or if the class pooh-poohs it (hey, they're so secure that they're getting cocky now), I'll point out that the word is a good choice and explain why (admittedly, sometimes I have to reach a bit). If the student is stronger, I'll let her explain her choice, offering help if she flounders. At this point, they have already seen how elements such

---

[5] And, if responses are not immediately forthcoming, I explain that once everyone in the class has come up with a word and explained it, the class can leave for the day. The levels of enthusiasm (and the number of responses) immediately skyrocket.

as class, gender, and power have driven the poem, and, although they may not understand metaphor yet, they certainly grasp how the impact of class, gender and power affect college students, and how certain words are key to identifying these themes. (And, to make theme identification easier, I'll group thematically similar words together as I write them on the board: if "worship," "weak," and "mine," for example, are clustered together, the class will be more likely to work out the theme of power.)

They generally surprise me: from the entire rich vocabulary of the poem, one young man chose the word "it," and I figured him for a smart-aleck. He then proceeded to point out that the poem was really about Porphyria's change from a "she" to an "it." I know full professors who wouldn't have picked that word out; certainly *I* never had. And of course, it was a wonderful choice which allowed me to introduce Browning's critique of female objectification and reification.

Okay. That sort of thing doesn't happen every time. Yet even the slowest students gradually come to realize that the poem is about *far* more than a sociopath who strangles his girlfriend.

Finishing "Porphyria," the class is upbeat and enthusiastic; they have a lot less fear about the next meeting, and some students even ask if we can "do" another poem then—"but a good one, like this; not one of the dumb ones." I'm way ahead of them; their next text will be Browning's "My Last Duchess," another creepy little poem about a sociopath who has his wife murdered. (I've included this poem in Appendix 1 as well.) And now learning really starts to take place.

> "Nine tenths of education is encouragement."
>
> — Anatole France

After I read "My Last Duchess" aloud—*even before we have begun to do any close reading*—there invariably is a silence, and someone, usually in the back, will mutter, "Shit, it's the same damn poem." Which, thematically, it is; but the level of literary sophistication required to recognize that fact is generally expected only in upper-level undergraduate students. My class is generally amazed by itself. Success is heady stuff — perhaps the most positive reinforcer of all.

So we've done it! The reading of a poem was a non-negative experience, even a positive experience for some (perhaps their first in an English class); they exercised the rudiments of close reading and learned how to isolate a theme; they've compared two works and recognized thematic similarities — and they did it employing canonical texts. Most importantly, they've started to overcome their "natural" aversion. "Okay," admitted one young man, still exhilarated by his realization that the late Porphyria and the Duchess' painting are both artifacts that the speakers prefer to actual women: "not *all* poems are stupid."

Pure Positive Reinforcement cannot go on forever, of course. Gradually, I must wean them from the constant stream of quarters, using techniques I'll explain later in the book. Gradually, we get to more difficult poems — although these poems will always be presented as puzzles to be solved (triggering their prey drives, enjoyment of competition, and quest for status). Gradually, they'll begin to write essays and introduce their own ideas into the discussion. *But none of this can happen until the "natural" aversion is overcome.*

"Play is the only way
the highest
intelligence
of humankind can
unfold."

— Joseph Chilton
Pearce

Once natural aversion is overcome, however, the fun *really* starts.

2
Positive Reinforcement Strategies

"This woman is such a loser. I came to college to get answers,
and all she ever does is ask questions."

— Anonymous student,
class evaluation, First-Year Seminar, 1989

P ositive reinforcement should be a part of every teacher's strategic arsenal: used in the proper context, and given the proper reinforcer, it's highly motivational; used correctly, it shapes precise behavior.

But there are pitfalls.

Be very careful: indeed, like virtually any tool, PPR can be misused; if not executed correctly (if the student doesn't really want the proffered reward, or if your timing is off, or if the sought-after behavior is vague or unfocussed), PPR can have exactly the opposite effect of that desired.

2.1 Relativity

*R*einforcers are relative. As I pointed out earlier, what you might perceive as a reward might be a punishment for someone else (remember Folly's piece of raw liver?). If, for example, I decide to use praise as a reinforcer, and I walk up to a linebacker who has given an answer in English class for what might be the first time in his life, what happens when I say "Why, *Al*bert, I am *so* very proud of you! What a *good* job!"?

What happens is that kissing and sucking noises will immediately buzz throughout the class and poor "Albert" will spend the rest of his undergraduate years being mercilessly teased, ducking hallway comments such as: "Why *Al*bert! I am *so* very proud of you for being *such* a suck-up! What a *good* boy!" This is the sort of "reward Alfie Kohn calls "coercion," and quite correctly dismisses as an aversive. Since it comes from a superior and is offered as a bribe, it both diminishes the recipient as an inferior, and signals to his peers that he is willing to accept—and trade on—his own inferiority. No wonder he is derided.

But if I instead stride up to the kid's desk and cry "Yess!! Way to go *Taz*!" ("Taz" is his nickname, used because he loathes the name Albert, and wishes to be thought of as The Tasmanian Devil) and slam two quarters down with a bang, we're functioning as colleagues who have solved a problem together. The quarter is *information*, a marker of his success. He'll probably offer me a high five (which I'll return) and his classmates will mutter, "Way to go, man!" It's happened before.

Many times.

2.2 Timing

A nother tremendously important part of positive reinforcement is timing. Good reinforcers are—indeed, must be—immediate: if the timing is even a few seconds late, the teacher will reinforce the wrong behavior. If I wish to reinforce a dog's straight sit, for example, but wait a beat or two too long, the dog may have shifted position by the time she receives her treat. Way to go, Darb. I've just reinforced a crooked sit, and will probably have to spend the remainder of the training session *un*reinforcing it. The longer the delay, the more useless—and sometimes even counterproductive —the reinforcer.

Perhaps the very worst reinforcer a teacher can rely upon is the final grade. Such grades are quite simply too far removed from the student's effort to be useful. Consider the student who has spent the entire semester goofing off, cutting classes, turning in papers late or not at all, barely passing exams. Suddenly, a week before the end of classes—*when there is suddenly a direct link between classwork and grade*—she begins to haunt your office and stalk you in the halls, motivated beyond belief: "Can I do some extra credit work? Will you allow me to retake that exam? Will you accept rewrites?" Had that been her attitude throughout the semester, she'd be acing the class. But the reward (or punishment) of the final grade only has weight when it is imminent. And by then it's too late.

> "The joy of learning is as indispensable in study as breathing is in running. Where it is lacking there are no real students, but only poor caricatures of apprentices who, at the end of their apprenticeship, will not even have a trade."
>
> — Simone Weil

2.3 Focus

Reinforcers must be focused on a specific behavior—and on only one behavior at a time. If my students are writing essays, and I wish to make them aware of their audience, I'll reinforce readable titles—and nothing else. In a very short time, papers with headings such as "My Essay" are rewritten with titles such as "The Day I Mooned my Second Grade Teacher." The rest of the essay doesn't matter, for now. Once the titles are consistently interesting, we'll move on to the first line, and I'll reinforce that. Unfocussed reinforcers are virtually useless. If I tell my teenaged daughter, "Be good today and you and your friends can use the car tonight," I'm setting us both up for disappointment and frustration. My idea of "being good" probably differs considerably from hers: I'm expecting a cleaned room, a tidy house, and freshly washed dishes; she's assuming that not burning down the house will be sufficient. In order for the reinforcer to be effective, she has to know *precisely* what I'm looking for.

2.4 Reinforcement: Something the Student Wants ...

A s I pointed out earlier, positive reinforcement must be something the student REALLY wants—the more the student wants it, the stronger the reinforcer. If the dog is bored with cheese, I use chicken. Bored with chicken? Try liver. Or perhaps the dog is not what trainers call a "foodie." My collie colleague Solo (so named because he was the only one in his litter) will work MUCH harder (and with much more enthusiasm) for a thrown tennis ball or a game of tug than for the tenderest piece of steak. If students have lost interest in quarters, let the ones doing the best work leave class ten minutes early (they don't need the practice).

In any case, the effectiveness of the motivation will be directly relative to the student's desire for the reinforcer.

2.5 … or Wants to Avoid

Negative reinforcement (details in section 3 below) is another extremely powerful tool. Dogs will stay inside electronic boundaries because a non-painful alarm on their collar warns them of mild pain to come if they wander past property lines.[6] Students will work like, well, *dogs* in order to avoid the horror of embarrassment in front of their peers. But beware of confusing negative reinforcement with punishment (3.1). Negative reinforcement is based on student *control*, punishment on student *helplessness*.

---

[6] Although one particularly clever Border Collie I know learned that if he simply lies down when the alarm goes off and waits until it stops (*i.e.,* waits for the bleeping battery to run down and quit) he can violate all boundaries with impunity. Alphas are clever. And patient.

2.6 Life Beyond PPR; or, B.F. Skinner Goes to the Dogs

> "Jesus, you must spend a fortune on us every week in quarters. And teachers don't make that much. Is your husband like really rich, or what?"

—Student inquiry,
English 215, 2003

Although the Pure Positive Reinforcement I use to combat "natural" aversion in my "Lit for Linebackers" class is wonderful as far as it goes, I'll be the first to admit that it doesn't go far enough—either in dog training or classroom teaching.

Admittedly, it's thrilling to work with a dog who leaps with joy when the training lead comes out, or a jubilant class that thinks you and your course are the best things since buttered popcorn. You might be tempted to keep on pushing PPR indefinitely; it's such a pleasant feel-good way to deal with things.

But you can't. Life just isn't that easy. Nor should it be.

As many psychologists and teachers have pointed out, PPR has two well-documented disadvantages when used over any length of time. **First**, it tends to focus the student on the reward rather than the task—everyone's so busy trying to score the next quarter that they lose sight of the larger view required for a full understanding of the material—or on the need to improve their intellectual skills. Keep feeding your dog cookies for staying at your side and she'll work reliably, but always at the same level—she won't, for example, look for nuances in your pace or try to anticipate changes in direction. Keep feeding students quarters for raising their hands and the hands will continue to pop up—but the quality of the answers won't improve.

Second, PPR loses impact quickly: the twentieth piece of liver never tastes as good as the first (even if you actually *like* liver); and, after the twelfth or thirteenth quarter, why push oneself to get a fourteenth?

The cookie-pusher school of dog training discovered these drawbacks early on: once food was removed from the equation (*i.e.*, in the show ring, where treats of any sort (even something as benign as verbal praise) is forbidden during exercises) the dogs often (okay, usually) lost interest in any sort of work and drifted off toward ringside in search of kids with potato chips.

Clearly, the animals were working for the reward, not the pleasure of the task.

Even when the dog was training at home, where the cookies kept coming on a fairly regular basis, the cookie-pusher's overstuffed dogs began belching and turning up their noses at anything less than sirloin. The trainer/trainee paradigm had become totally inverted: instead of the dog learning to increase the precision of his work, the trainer was being conditioned to increase the quality of the reinforcer.

How could positive reinforcement be maintained once the cookies stopped? And how could the initial impact of the PPR be maintained, with or without cookies? Dog trainers muddled through for a while, usually trying to trick their dogs into working at dog shows by pretending that food was *just* on the way. Smart dogs figured out the ruse almost immediately; even the dimmer bulbs took only two or three shows to discover the awful truth.

So the dog trainers, many of whom had once had introductory psychology classes in college, went home or to the library, and dug out dusty volumes of B. F. Skinner.

And, although behaviorism was no longer trendy in the colleges, and although dog trainers had never swallowed the Skinnerian notion that their beloved companion was only a fertilized canine egg's way to create another fertilized canine egg,[7] the psychologist still provided trainers with useful strategies to deal with the PPR problem. Indeed, the strategies were so effective that they found themselves having an entirely new and much more enjoyable relationship with their dogs: a relationship based not upon control and submission or bribery, but on shared responsibility and mutual satisfaction.

Here's what they discovered.

---

[7] "A hen is just an egg's way of producing another egg": B.F. Skinner.

2.7 Selective and Variable Reinforcement

Constant reinforcement—"cookie pushing" for dogs, a steady stream of quarters for students—should only be used during *very* early learning stages or to overcome "natural" aversion.

As the student gains facility and confidence, the teacher should gradually begin to use longer and longer "schedules": that is, increase the time between rewards. Positive reinforcement is replaced with *selective* reinforcement: when hands are readily raised on a regular basis, for example, I no longer reinforce just any answer at all—it has to be a good one. When all the answers are good, only the terrific ones are reinforced. The quarter moves from being a reward to being information: a marker indicating that significant progress has been made toward solving a problem.

Although it might seem counter-intuitive, the delay actually encourages improvement: the longer the schedule, the more powerful the motivator. Go figure.

For teachers, the important exception to this delaying tactic is rewarding the response to a puzzle or an exam. These must be rewarded promptly each time: making students wait for improvement is encouraging; making them wait to find out if they're right or not is just frustrating.

2.8 Conditioned Reinforcement

A conditioned reinforcer comes in two flavors: primary, and secondary. Folly's primary reinforcer is a cookie. For a student, it's a quarter.

A primary reinforcer is something real, something you can hold in your hand (or, if you're a dog, something you can eat). A secondary reinforcer is a delayed reinforcement: it's symbolic; it's information; it's an indication that the student is on the right track and a reward is on its way, but it's not here just quite yet—the student will have to work just a little longer to get it.

When I train dogs, I employ a clicker as a secondary reinforcer—no, not the glitzy handheld gadgets that many of today's students use to respond to classroom polls and quizzes, but the old-fashioned  crickety-sounding handheld noisemakers that nuns used to use in Catholic school when you were being too noisy—right before they rapped your knuckles with a ruler. They used it as a warning, but it's just as powerful when used as a promise. Folly's clicker tells her that she's doing the *right* thing, and that if she continues, she'll accomplish her goal and receive her reward. Even though it might seem to be a form of delay, the feedback it provides is instantaneous, focusing on the specific behavior leading up to the completion of a task.

Let's say I hide a glove somewhere in a room and ask Folly to find it. Without moving, without saying anything, without doing anything but clicking the secondary reinforcer, I can direct her to the hiding place (my hints work on the same principle as the "you're getting warmer" game that children play). And Folly will work eagerly and persistently, enjoying the process of finding her "prey," using the clicks as information while looking forward to her reward—which she is absolutely certain will come once she's solved the problem I've given her. Audiences who watch her work are particularly impressed by her persistence and unremitting enthusiasm even during a long and presumably frustrating search.

Whether one calls it a conditioned reinforcer or a secondary reinforcer, it promotes long-term work. Try it with students: tantalize them with a quarter dangled just out of their reach as they expand their answers. The delay will increase their motivation to keep working (as long as they realize that if they keep expanding their answer, they'll eventually get the quarter). They understand conditioned reinforcers: after all, they've been reared in a society where people work endlessly for money, a secondary reinforcer for things money can buy. (One could argue that the quarters I give students could actually be perceived as secondary reinforcers, since the coins themselves have no innate value, after all. You can't eat them or wear them. But they *are* primary reinforcers in my class, since they are trophies of a sort, and grant instant **status** — which I'll discuss later.)

As long as the CR always leads to tangible reward, and is reserved for a "real" task (a specific, realizable goal), it is highly effective. (Note — this strategy is particularly useful and effective when dealing with student papers. See the section on prewrites and "teachable moments" in section 3.1 below.)

"Education is what survives when what has been learned has been forgotten."

— B. F. Skinner

"Education is what remains when we have forgotten all that we have been taught."

— George Savile, Marquis of Halifax

"Education is what remains after one has forgotten everything he learned in school."

- Albert Einstein

2.9 Jackpots

S everal years ago, one of my quieter students (okay, it was the sixth week and she'd said *nothing* in class so far) had an epiphany and came up with a beautiful, elegant reading of the closing lines of a poem. I patted my pockets for quarters, and to my horror found out I was without one. Digging through my book bag, I found a ten-dollar bill I'd been saving for lunch money and slapped it on the student's desk.

That ten-dollar bill was the best money I have ever spent, pedagogically speaking. It has become something of a legend on my campus, and students are still waiting for another one to appear.

A jackpot—for a dog, a quarter pound of meat given at once, for a student, a handful of quarters dumped on her desk—can be earned or unearned. In the case of the ten-dollar student, it was used to mark a sudden breakthrough; I've also used it to motivate an unwilling, fearful, or resistant student who makes any sort of effort, however tentative.

I might not produce a sawbuck for a student who raises her hand for the first time in the fifth week of class, but she's darned well going to get a lot more than one lousy quarter.

3
Negative Reinforcement: the Darker Side of PPR?

Teacher: "Really nice presentation. Much better than last time."

Student: "Well, *duh*. What else was I supposed to do? No way I was going to look like a jerk again."

— Conversation,
English 314 (Romantic Literature) 1995

Negative reinforcement is the most frequently misunderstood aspect of behavioral conditioning. If I give Folly a cookie because she sat on command, everyone understands the concept: that's positive reinforcement, right?: no problem. But what if I give her a cookie for *not* picking on the cat? Positive or negative reinforcement? And what if I beat her (yeah, right) for going into the garbage—negative *something*, sure. But is it reinforcement? Or punishment? And what's the difference between the two? Okay. I'll start with a definition, and then give you some examples.

Negative reinforcement means that something you don't want to happen—what psychologists would call an "aversive event"—will indeed *not* happen if you modify your behavior. The goal of negative reinforcement is to increase the likelihood of the specific behavior in the future.

If you're still confused, the following story should help clear things up.

My favorite example of negative reinforcement took place in Montreal, where Folly and I were doing a workshop. On the day I had put aside for sightseeing, we went for a walk in the Old City — surely one of the loveliest places in the world. Folly, being a dog, had to relieve herself, and I, being a responsible dog owner, took one of the plastic bags I always carry in my pockets, leaned over, and picked up her … leavings. I sealed the bag carefully and looked about for a garbage can.

Montreal is an exquisite city, but it has an absolute dearth of garbage bins. I have no idea how they manage to keep the place so impeccably clean. With no receptacle in sight, I neatly tucked the bag in my jacket pocket (no, this story is *not* going where you think it is), and Folly and I continued our walk. We came to a large open plaza, where a free jazz festival was in progress, and I spotted a trash bin on the far side. Weaving in and out through the crowds, we finally arrived at the garbage can and I reached into my pocket to retrieve the bag of poop.

The bag was gone.

I had been pickpocketed.

I often wonder what that poor thief must have thought when he went to open his purloined treasure. Probably that Americans were *very* weird. Possibly, he considered another line of work. I certainly hope so.

That's negative reinforcement.

You see, no one *forced* the pickpocket to go after me. It was his choice, just as the choice to change professions would be his.

Negative reinforcement is an aversive conditioner that is **based entirely upon on student control**—the aversive can be halted or avoided altogether the moment that the student decides to change the unwanted behavior.

Let's say I have a student who consistently shows up to class five or ten minutes late. I don't want to scold or nag him and upset the rather tenuous working relationship we've developed; I don't want to threaten and become a policeman; and I don't want to quibble over just how late he is or just how much he can get away with and become a parent. I just want him to *want* to show up on time and monitor himself.

But how can I make him want to do something he clearly *doesn't* want to do? Negative reinforcement. Here's how it works.

> "The illiterate of the 21st century will not be those who cannot read and write, but those who cannot learn, unlearn, and relearn. "
>
> — Alvin Toffler

First, I check with the school registrar and find out when and where his class before mine is held. No problem there—it's about two minutes away. Turns out he's been ducking outside for a smoke between classes. So, I inform the class (while he's present) that I'm going to begin giving brief and very simple quizzes at the beginning of each class, so that I'll be able to determine who has done the reading and who hasn't (no mention of timeliness). I explain that I'll also use the quizzes as a form of roll-taking, to save time. Students who aren't there to take the quiz will receive an "F" on it, which will be averaged into their class participation grade, and they will be counted absent unless they come up to me after class (since I have a fairly strict attendance policy, the absence is a real concern).

End of problem. Suddenly it becomes the *student's* responsibility to show up on time; otherwise he'll not only have to take the F, but interact with me after class in order to establish his attendance — and, indirectly, his tardiness. It's negative reinforcement; therefore I'm not stuck being the bad guy or the policeman or the parent.

If he takes the F, he can't really be angry with *me*; it was his own decision to grab a few last puffs, after all. Everyone *else* in the class got there on time. And, most importantly, ***the negative reinforcement of his poor grade will stop immediately when his new behavior begins.*** He understands precisely why bad things are happening, and precisely what he can do to make them stop happening.

This particular negative reinforcer — the daily quiz — has become a regular part of my classroom procedure because of additional benefits I hadn't even considered when working out my negative reinforcement strategy. Not only does it assure student promptness, but it motivates the class to do the assigned reading. The questions are simple, but require at least minimal comprehension (if I ask what the Ancient Mariner had around his neck, a random guess is unlikely to produce an albatross). I now have a daily record of who's doing the reading and who isn't. An added benefit is that the BS artists in the class, who are perfectly capable of gleaning enough information from their classmates' remarks on the material for some ad lib discussion, are exposed as phonies. Best of all, they (ahem) expose *themselves*.

Students who fail the quizzes are embarrassed (as they should be), but not devastated — this is a quiz, not an exam, and there are a lot of them. The stakes are small, since an "F" on a single day's quiz has absolutely no impact their final grade — they'd have to blow a *lot* of quizzes for that to happen. But they still wish to avoid the embarrassment, and as a result, they begin to prepare more carefully. When they do so, the "Ds" and "Fs" immediately turn into "As."

The result is student confidence, student pride, and student self-motivation. And an added benefit! if they've actually *done* the reading, they're far more willing (and far more able) to contribute intelligently to class discussion.

3.1 Punishment: Too Much, Too Late

Negative reinforcement is *not* punishment. Indeed, the two are diametrically opposed to one another. Negative reinforcement is based on student power. Punishment is based on student powerlessness—no changes the student attempts to make in behavior will affect the outcome.

My veterinarian was called to the local pound to examine a three-month old Rottweiler puppy with two broken hips, whose owner had slammed him repeatedly against a brick wall to make him "meaner." The puppy had no idea what was happening; he had no idea what "mean" even *meant*. Thus there was nothing he could do to escape the brutality. Students—or people in general, for that matter—can find themselves in less physical but similarly terrifying situations.

> "It is little short of a miracle that modern methods of instruction have not already completely strangled the holy curiosity of inquiry. I believe that one could even deprive a healthy beast of prey of its voraciousness if one could force it with a whip to eat continuously whether it were hungry or not."
>
> — Albert Einstein

> "Just as eating against one's will is injurious to health, so studying without a liking for it spoils the memory, and it retains nothing it takes in."
>
> - Leonardo Da Vinci

Let's say, for example, that my pickpocket had exhausted every other means of earning a living—that he had been reduced to picking pockets as a matter of sheer survival. In that case, my poop-filled bag would not have been negative reinforcement, but punishment: nothing more than one of Fate's crueler jokes. The incident would have taught him nothing.

Similarly, let's say my student was late to class not because he was downstairs smoking, but because he had a broken ankle and was on crutches—or because his previous class was on the other side of campus—and he could not physically make it to class on time *no matter how hard he tried*. In that case, giving him an "F" for missing a quiz at the beginning of class would have been nothing more than punishment.

Perhaps the best example of student punishment is a low final grade given when the class is over.

I discovered that such grades were punishment in the process of well-intentioned effort: I used to spend twenty or thirty precious end-of-semester hours marking final papers, pointing out grammatical problems, flaws in logic and organization and so forth. I found it extremely disheartening to discover, when I returned to my office the following fall, that virtually none of the papers had even been picked up, much less examined for commentary. Yet why should they have been? The grade had been given. There was nothing the student could do at that point to change it. Why bother?

In this case, *timing* is everything—and can make the difference between student control and student impotence. Merely changing the timing of my critique can change it from useless punishment to motivational negative aversion. Here's how.

I no longer mark up final papers.

Instead, I make it a point to use what Barbara Walvoord terms the "teachable moment." Well before final papers are due, I ask students to submit "prewrites" that I mark and hand back to them *before the paper receives a final grade.* Suddenly I find that my scrawled notes are not ignored, but read and re-read like pieces of scripture— after all, it's a direct explication of specific things that the student can do that will actually make a difference in the final grade. **A prewrite "F" ceases to be worthless punishment and turns into helpful negative reinforcement when I tell the student precisely how she can raise the grade:** a student can turn in a prewrite or choose to take her chances; if she does turn one in, she can rewrite or not rewrite. It's all totally in her control. And if she gets an "F," it was *her* choice to do so.

> "'Reeling and Writhing, of course, to begin with,' the Mock Turtle replied [to the question of what was taught in school], 'and then the different branches of Arithmetic - Ambition, Distraction, Uglification, and Derision.'"
>
> —Lewis Carroll (*Alice's Adventures in Wonderland*)

Punishment can occur *during* the semester as well, however. Suppose a student is failing a class at midterm, and suppose she has been doing poorly on papers and exams because of her own confusion about how to write and study. In her view, she has "worked hard" but papers are still coming back marked with "Ds" and "Fs". With no idea of how improve things—with no idea of how to escape what she perceives as punishment, the student will act—well, like a dog. If the punishment does not cease—and it won't, because she has no idea how to *make* it stop—she will follow a predictable canine series of behaviors: flight, fight, submission, and shutdown.

Her first attempt to escape the punishment will be flight. Just as any sensible dog will try to run away from a beating, most students will drop the class that's beating them up. In either case, education has failed to take place. But what if it's too late in the semester to drop? Or the parents insist that the student finish out a class that has, after all, already been paid for? At least one form of flight is still an option: students will start cutting classes and missing meetings with their professor; they'll no longer even bother to pick up their papers—or even write them, for that matter. It's denial, of course, but at least the student is temporarily avoiding her own helplessness—and the punishment.

Of course, she's not really escaping. I can put a strong leather lead on a dog, so that he can't run away. And I can enforce an attendance policy in my classes, and call my student's advisor and/or parents—she'll quickly be brought back to heel.

With no available avenue of escape, a dog will panic and begin to fight back. A student will grow hostile and angry. She won't contribute to class discussions; she might be disruptive. She might complain to the dean or her parents that I am unfair and am singling her out for abuse.

But that won't work either. I can muzzle a dog so that it cannot bite me, and then continue to beat the poor animal. The dean is unlikely to see the student's side of things. Professor Lewes is, he assures her, a tough but fair person, and if the student will just work harder, she is certain to succeed. Her parents will tell her to stop complaining and just do the work. Of course, the problem is that the poor kid doesn't know *how* to do the work. And the punishment keeps on coming.

Both the dog and the student will now move into a submissive phase, desperately trying to appease their punisher, desperately trying to figure out what on earth this person wants. The trapped dog will roll over, beg, sit: frantically offering every kind of behavior it can think of to appease its trainer's anger. The trapped student will act in much the same way. This is the point when plagiarism often crops up—not the haphazard effort of a lazy student, but the panicked response of a terrified one, who quite honestly does not understand what the teacher wants or how to escape the punishment of failure.

But let's say that the dog's efforts are fruitless; the trainer will not be appeased. Or the student is caught with her stolen paper. Finally, the worst happens: total shutdown. The dog collapses, zones out, and further beatings have no effect. It will offer no resistance; it can be beaten to death at this point. The student may drop out of school altogether; in particularly terrible cases when dropping out is not seen as an option, she might attempt suicide; in the worst, she might succeed.

Fortunately, very few situations involving student punishment are this extreme, but when one considers that punishment can so easily be reworked into negative reinforcement, such instances seem not only useless, but also cruel.

3.2 No Reward Marker

In addition to positive and negative reinforcement, trainers and teachers can make use of the no-reward marker. We all have employed it at one time or another—even very young children use it. Remember when you used to play the game of "you're getting warmer?" You didn't rely purely on positive reinforcement. Your playmates found the object a *lot* faster if they knew when they were getting "colder" as well. "Colder" is not positive reinforcement, nor is it negative reinforcement. It's neutral, there only for the purpose of transmitting information. It does not mean "you have the wrong answer," but rather "you might as well save your strength—it's a blind alley."

4
Behavior Shaping:
Performance without Pain

"Once I knew what I was expected to do, it was a **lot** easier to do it."

—Student comment,
Victorian Literature, 1996

N o one, I am certain, can write a book. I know that I can't. Yet I *can* write a sentence. And I can arrange several sentences into a paragraph, and several paragraphs into a chapter. And so forth. Eventually, I'll have my book.

The same process works for dogs and students, but—of course—I'll begin with dogs. In advanced American Kennel Club obedience, there is an exercise called the "scent discrimination retrieve." Ten dumbbells—five made of leather, five of metal—are placed about twenty feet in front of the dog, who must go out and find the one with the owner's scent, and retrieve it. The dog must make this selection based on scent alone.

A dog might be able to complete this exercise without training, although it's unlikely: she might have an incredible nose and love both retrieving and her owner so much that she'll bring back the correct dumbbell just because it has the beloved scent on it. Or she might luck into grabbing the right one.

Similarly, a student might have a natural gift for writing and love the subject I'm teaching, and write a brilliant paper. Or a student might be lucky enough — like one of those hypothetical monkeys who accidentally types *Hamlet* — to stumble into a good paper.

But it would be unreasonable to expect such things from all of our students — indeed, even from most of them — on a regular basis.

Dog trainers assume — quite rightly — that no dog can successfully complete the scent discrimination exercise on a regular basis without training. And trainers understand that attempting to train the entire exercise all at once would be overwhelming for the dog, and thus futile. That's because the scent retrieve isn't just one behavior, but rather a set of linked behaviors. And the scent retrieve itself will later be combined with other skills — sit at heel, return to front, return to heel, and so forth — to make an even more complex exercise which requires all forty-or-so elements to be combined and performed correctly for a passing score.

So we take our large goal and break it down into a series of feasible intermediate tasks. For example, we must first teach the dog to retrieve. But even that preliminary skill needs to be broken down into individual tasks such as holding the dumbbell (as opposed to spitting it out at our feet), and surrendering it on command (as opposed to turning the exercise into a game of "tug"). And, most importantly, the task must be broken down into manageable tasks that the student — human or canine — can complete and understand.

Here's the scent retrieve:

Steps to Train a Scent Retrieve

1. Dog holds forefinger in mouth unwillingly
2. Dog holds forefinger willingly
3. Dog opens mouth for forefinger
4. Dog reaches for forefinger
5. Dog holds paper roll
6. Dog reaches for paper roll
7. Dog picks up paper roll
8. Dog holds dumbbell
9. Dog reaches for dumbbell
10. Dog picks up dumbbell from 2, 4, 6, 8, 10, 12 feet
11. Dog retrieves dumbbell next to unscented anchored leather article
12. Dog holds leather article
13. If averse to leather, desensitize
14. Dog reaches for leather article
15. Dog picks up leather article
16. Dog picks up leather article from 2, 4, 6, 10, 12 feet
17. Dog retrieves leather article next to unscented leather article
18. Dog holds metal article
19. Dog reaches for metal article
20. Dog picks up metal article from 2, 4, 6, 8, 10, 12 feet
21. If averse to metal, desensitize
22. Dog retrieves metal article next to unscented anchored metal article
23. Dog retrieves leather article next to unscented anchored metal and leather article
24. Next to unscented anchored leather and two unscented metal
25. Dog retrieves metal article next to unscented anchored metal and leather article
26. Dog retrieves metal article next to unscented anchored metal and two unscented leather
27. Dog retrieves metal article next to gradually increasing combinations of anchored unscented metal and leather up to 10 unscented articles
28. Gradual removal of anchors—if dog retrieves unscented article, repeat steps 19 to 24 as needed
29. Introduction of "cold" vs. "hot" scent
30. Introduction of foreign scent
31. Dog does scent retrieve in distracting area

Step one is to teach the dog to hold the handler's forefinger in her mouth. The finger is used—rather than a pencil or other solid object—because the trainer has more control over the finger, and because the finger holds the scent that will eventually be the basis for the exercise. The dog will be unwilling at first, but the trainer will heavily reward the behavior until the dog moves to step two: holding the forefinger willingly. And so on, all the way down to step thirty-one. Then the trainer combines the straight sit-in-front, the delivery, and the return to correct heel position next to the handler.

Any dog—no matter how old, young, bright, stubborn, or stupid—can learn this trick (or "behavior," in techno-dog speak). And, if taught in appropriate sequence, and if each step along the way is heavily reinforced, *any* dog can learn the entire process (assuming that he has not lost his powers of scent through illness or accident).

Along the way, there is a careful gradual reduction in repetition and increase in quality. When Folly demonstrates step one at workshops and is rewarded for holding my finger, she looks at me as if I were mad and seems vaguely embarrassed about receiving a reward for such a puppyish skill. (But she still accepts the cookie.)

For a dog, the scent discrimination exercise is the rough equivalent of a term paper: a task requiring the mastery of several apparently non-associated tasks brought together into a unified whole. It's not easy—some particularly slow or stubborn dogs will take a year or two to put everything together. Yet any dog can learn to perform

> "It should be possible to explain the laws of physics to a barmaid."
>
> — Albert Einstein

the scent retrieve — *as long as each specific task is selectively reinforced* (see 2.7, above) *along the way.*

Yes, even old, "stupid," "stubborn" dogs. Even **your** dog. Follow the rubric above and you'll see.

Human beings can be "trained" in much the same way. Any student — no matter how old, young, bright or stupid or stubborn, can learn the "trick" of writing an essay or solving a complex mathematical theorem if the teacher reduces the exercise to a series of feasible tasks, takes those tasks in proper sequence, and heavily reinforces each step along the way.

Of course, coming up with the proper set of feasible tasks is not easy. Indeed, in doing so the teacher may realize that because of her own interest in and comfort with her discipline, she has "skipped" a few steps in the exercise — a Golden retriever would probably never need the first few steps in the rubric above; a Bloodhound would get the "discrimination" part with little or no help. Students are similarly various in ability.

Yet for the scent discrimination rubric to work, it must list *every* step, so that *every* dog can follow it — Golden Retrievers, Border Collies, Poodles, Bloodhounds, even Afghans.

Same thing for students. Teachers must be sure that they are starting at the very *very* beginning, and missing no steps in between. An incomplete or incorrect process can destroy the entire fabric of the student-teacher relationship along with the student's ability to

succeed in the class. And each step in the process must be small enough so that student can follow it and be reinforced.

For example: most students write papers because they must. Can't pass the class without writing them. Papers are an otherwise useless, but absolutely unavoidable evil. Or so the students think.

So my first step is to make them aware that there is an actual *reader* out there, and that the reason one writes a paper is not to pass the class, but to inform or entertain that reader. For me, that sort of awareness is the most fundamental aspect of writing, so that's where I begin.

Step one in my rubric is not "choosing a topic" or "doing library research." It's a task that's simple enough for any student to manage: learning how to craft a lively title that will engage a reader. The topic is secondary; it may or may not flow out of the title; that's not important at this point. What is important— essential—is for students to imagine themselves in the reader's place: what title would interest *me*? What title would make *me* want to proceed to the first line of the essay? "Essay #2"? Or "The Day I Died"? "Paper #4"? Or "Meeting an Alien from the Planet Elvis"? "My Essay"? Or "How to Break Your Leg"?

> "A good education is the next best thing to a pushy mother."
>
> — Charles Schulz

When grades are given purely for the title, I immediately stop getting papers headed "My Prom," and start getting ones such as "The Night My Boyfriend Threw Up on the Chauffeur" (see below). I don't worry about thesis, organization, spelling or punctuation at this point. To do so would only cause confusion. I teach only *one* aspect of the final product at a time. And for me, reader awareness is Aspect One. Step One. Job One.

It doesn't really matter how the steps are arranged — your first step might be my third — just that they are all there and follow a logical progression that *any* student who has qualified for First-Year Whatever-your-subject-is can understand.

Only when my students have completely grasped the idea of a title that appeals to an audience — in short, when they've moved successfully to a schedule of variable reinforcement and are turning out provocative titles on a regular basis — will I move on to the next step. That step will vary from class to class: in a beginning composition class, for example, they might try to remember an event in their lives that a *reader* might find interesting.

Adolescents are of course generally a bit egocentric and most find it difficult to grasp the notion of reader reaction: for the first assignment, I'll usually get a self-centered stack of papers which can be divided roughly into "My Prom" (typical opening line: "John looked so handsome in his tuxedo as the limo drove up"); or "The Big Game" ("All of us knew that this was the most important game of the season").

When I continue to reinforce an awareness of the reader, however, students begin to realize that — just as a title such as "My Essay" is not inherently interesting to anyone except the writer's Mom (who has a personal interest in the writer), a perfect prom or a winning championship game is not inherently interesting to someone who was not there and has no personal stake in the matter. Students will rethink their topics and start coming up with more universally appealing subjects such as the awful moment they learned about

Santa ("My parents were liars!"), or realized their own mortality ("As I stood at the top of the steep slope, I began to wish I had taken skiing lessons").

Example: in a workshop session, Student A realizes that no one is particularly interested in reading her essay about her graduation, an idyllic day filled with loving hugs, tears, and countless photographs. Learning takes place: after reading a Student B's similar account of her own graduation, Student A realizes that even *she* isn't interested in the topic as such. What to do? What will her classmates want to read about? Well, as it turns out, Student A just happens to have endured the Prom From Hell. When she mentions said Prom in class to her workshop group, interest is immediate: "He showed up *drunk*? My God! What on earth did you *do*?" And the essay entitled "The Night My Boyfriend Threw Up on the Chauffeur" is born.

Example: in his workshop group, Student C realizes that no one is particularly interested in how his team won the state Lacrosse championship. But everyone wants the details of how his high school biology frog cadaver wound up in the biology teacher's desk drawer. Hence the essay "The Frog Who Wouldn't Die."

Then we'll work on a first line:

"The morning that I discovered that my frog was missing, I began to fear that I would never pass biology."

I'll bet even *you* want to read the essay now.

It is only at this point—well after the notion of reader awareness is firmly in place—that I'll have the student work on a thesis. Why *did* this particular event stick in his mind? Did he learn anything from the event? Could his readers learn anything from the event? As it turned out, in the case of the frog essay, the answer to both questions was "yes." His next step will be turning his learning process into a thesis (in this case, how an apparently negative event turned out to have a positive effect on his world view). We then deal with organization (chronological? flashback? one-act play?), and work on a conclusion.

While they're working on new concepts — a reader awareness topic, for example — I'll let my concern for earlier steps in the rubric slip for a bit. I won't worry about the title for now. Instead, my concern — and grade — will be directed to the new step. Juggling two tasks at once can be tricky for a beginner, after all. Only when students are starting to get "As" and "Bs" on their choice of topic (and courage resulting from a pattern of success), will we go back and try to find an equally stimulating title.

> "I won't say ours was a tough school, but we had our own coroner. We used to write essays like: What I'm going to be if I grow up."
>
> --Lennie Bruce

Flexibility is another key factor in behavior shaping: sometimes my canine or human students will dazzle me and move suddenly forward — another reason why I must have the entire rubric worked out before I begin. I have to be able to move forward with them, to travel at their pace, rather than my own.

Or sometimes a concept which the students had apparently mastered seems to disappear from their grasp. Again, I must be flexible: instead of getting angry, or insisting on bulling on ahead, dragging the class figuratively kicking and screaming behind me, I must be prepared to go back — and with no loss of enthusiasm or diminution of reinforcement. After all, I want to be able to end each training session — or classroom session — on an upbeat note, with the students feeling proud of themselves and willing (if not eager) to try again next time.

I used to dislike the rubric approach to teaching and grading. I found the idea of reducing the creation of an essay to a schematic roughly analogous to assembling a carburetor distasteful at best.

But then I realized that my privileging the act of successful essay writing exclusively to talented writers who did not need a rubric was as silly as arguing that only Golden Retrievers and Bloodhounds should be taught the scent discrimination exercise. Any dog could learn it, and have fun doing so—why deny them the opportunity?

Memoir:
Negotiating the Term Paper

T he first ten-page term paper I ever had to write was for an undergraduate "French Society and Culture" class. I was frozen with terror. What subject on earth, I wondered, could be so complex, so diverse, that it would require an entire *ten pages* to discuss? Finally I came up with a possibility. The title of my essay (ahem):

"French Literature"

Yup, French literature. *All* of it.

As you might expect, the essay was a bit, well, *superficial*. But my blessed French teacher didn't flunk me, nor give me a low grade and let me slip by. Instead, she sat me down and showed me how to write a ten-page paper. It is the model I used for the remainder of my undergraduate term papers, for my twenty-five page graduate seminar papers, for my fifty-page master's thesis, for my two-hundred page doctoral dissertation, and for several books (including this one).

Oddly enough, she referred me to one of the smallest models available: the five-paragraph essay. Intro, three body paragraphs, conclusion. Nothing scary; nothing overwhelming. Anyone could do it. Even me.

I could certainly use the model to write a three-to-five page essay. Thesis: "X is the case, and there are three reasons why." Simple. Intro (half page), one page devoted to each of the reasons, and a conclusion (half page). The breakthrough that she provided me was the fact that if I wrote three such essays on a single topic and combined them, I had a ten-page term paper!

Here's how it works. Let's say you must write an essay for my Romantic Literature course. I will have supplied a list of six to ten novels; you're to pick one by the fourth week of class. You decide that you'd like to write an essay on Jane Austen's *Pride and Prejudice* — you read it once before and remember that it wasn't *too* gross. You sit down and read it again, finishing the book by the sixth week of class.

Then you meet with me and we'll talk about the book. What did you like about it? Hate about it?

At the end of week seven, you must submit a five paragraph essay telling me what you particularly liked (or hated) about the book. You were fascinated by the characters of the three oldest sisters?

Why? It was interesting, you point out, how different the sisters were, even though they all came from the same family: Jane was very restrained, Lydia really wild, and Lizzie somewhere in the middle. When you write your five-paragraph essay on the topic, you do a sort of "Three Bears"/Aristotelian Golden Mean critique: Lydia Bennet is far too "hot" (passionate, impulsive), Jane Bennet is too "cold" (i.e., passive, submissive), but Elizabeth Bennet is "just right."[8] Intro, three body paragraphs, conclusion. Simple.

Next, why not try this: write an extended five paragraph essay (roughly three pages) proving that Lydia was indeed "too hot." Thesis: "Lydia is too wild and there are three reasons why I can say that this is so." Go into the book and find examples of her over-the-top nature (one page), note how others respond to her actions (one page), and examine the terrible effects her actions have on those around her (one page). With intro and conclusion, you've got three or four well-organized pages.

I'll write you a response paper (see Appendix 2). If you'd like, you can meet with me and we'll discuss the "chunk": its style, organization, argument, use of evidence, and so forth.

Then, put the Lydia essay aside for a bit. Try working on the "Jane" section instead. Working thesis: "Jane is too passive and there are three reasons why I can say this is so." Write a three-page essay on this topic. Find examples of her passive nature, and note how others respond to it. Passivity is going to cause different sorts of ripples: you may discover, for example, that it impacts mainly Jane and those closest to her. And you'll have a second three- or four-page "chunk."

---

[8] Admittedly, I've always had a problem with Southey's *Three Bears* story. If Mama Bear's medium-sized bowl of porridge was indeed "too cold," wouldn't Baby Bear's even smaller portion be even colder? (This sort of thing keeps many teachers awake at night.)

I'll write a second response paper, and schedule a required meeting with me, during which we'll discuss this "chunk" on its own merits, and in relation to the Lydia section.

Finally, subject Lizzie to the same sort of scrutiny. Threeish pages, same format. You decide in the process that Austen intends her as a normative character, and that one of the functions of *Pride and Prejudice* is as a conduct book for young ladies. What a great controlling thesis!

Another response paper, another meeting (if you'd like) and we'll discuss this "chunk" and its relationship to the other sections.

Assemble the three mini-essays, paying special attention to transitions, give the entire paper a solid rewrite, and you're done: your well-organized ten-page paper is a *fait accompli*. Since you handed in each "chunk" separately, we have had an ongoing discussion about the paper, textual evidence, organization, style, effective ways to present your arguments, and so forth. And it's all been done without terror or procrastination (and the overnight nightmare of a last-minute paper).

Sound like a dry way to be creative? Perhaps, if you're a gifted writer with a facility for natural organization. But if you're one of the rest of us, such a structured format gives us the time to actually think about what we're doing (and to change things that aren't coming out the way we wished them to), and the security to experiment with wit and humor, format, even thesis.

Which, some might argue, is exactly what creativity is all about. Face it: it's hard to invent an elegant new artsy swimming stroke if you're too busy drowning.

But now, back to the text.

U sing rubrics and carefully scheduled papers, I discovered that all my students could eventually learn to write a good, readable essay. And I discovered something else as well. I used to think my students were stupid and/or lazy when they turned in poorly written, boring, sloppily presented papers clearly put together at the last minute. When I established a firm set of criteria, however, and explained precisely what each student must do to receive an "A" or "B" on a paper, I suddenly found myself with a classroom full of "A" and "B" students. When I raised my standards and demanded (far) more, my students responded not with complaint, but by elevating their performance levels.

Eventually I realized that my "smart teacher and lazy/stupid class" paradigm was flat-out wrong. What I really had was an "unclear teacher and confused class" model. All I had to do was explain to the poor kids exactly what I wanted from them and they were more than willing to give their all.

Indeed, the most annoying thing about behavior shaping and a rubric approach to grading is probably just how well the damned system works.

4.1 "But isn't behaviorism just manipulation?"

"Of course, Behaviorism 'works.' So does torture. Give me a no-nonsense, down-to-earth behaviorist, a few drugs, and simple electrical appliances, and in six months I will have him reciting the Athanasian Creed in public."

—W. H. Auden

"But Darby," people at my workshops sometimes point out, "all this behavior modification and reinforcement is designed to work on a purely infantile level. College students are not children. Education is supposed to turn them into well-rounded adults, not trained poodles. How will they ever learn to think originally and creatively, to make their own decisions, to determine their own moral centers? And what happens when they leave this fully reinforced world? How on earth will they be prepared to face society as adults?"

I agree. But let me make three points.

First, behavior modification is everywhere: advertisements seductively suggesting the bliss of inhaling Marlboros, or chugging Budweisers, or wearing *Victoria's Secret* underwear; job promotions and pink slips; Mom's phone call way too early on Sunday morning asking when you're leaving for church.

As teachers, we are always reinforcing selected behaviors, as are students' friends, family, and employers: my point is that *as educators we should be particularly aware of what it is we're reinforcing and how we are reinforcing it.*

In one lecture course I attended as an undergrad, for example, I learned an extremely valuable skill — although probably not the one my instructor intended to teach. I learned how to get through a dull fifty-minute lecture while appearing attentive: you listen until the speaker says a word beginning with the letter "A," then "B," and so forth through the Alphabet (I generally allowed a word beginning with "ex" to stand for "X," and omitted "Z" — there were simply not enough xenophobes or zebras in my prof's lectures). It's a skill I still find occasionally useful at conferences and/or committee meetings.

When you're next suffering through a lecture whose subject is the rough equivalent of "A study of the causal relationship between groundward tropism and lachrimatory behavior forms in prematurated isolates" (translation: "Why kids cry when they fall down"), feel free to use it.

Second, behavior modification works. In workshops, I have seen multiple PhD holders, super-cool graduate students, and highly dignified academic administrators work (you should excuse the expression) like dogs to earn — yup, you guessed it — a quarter.

Finally, keep in mind that behavior modification is a means to an end, not the end in itself. It is quite simply the most effective way I have found to teach students how to acquire the skills necessary to succeed not only in their disciplines, but in their lives.

4.2 "And aren't rewards just bribes?"

Alfie Kohn is, of course, the author of many highly persuasive books arguing against competition, standardized testing, and reward. When I deliver the first half of my workshops (covering the material you've read so far), people tend to brandish his name like a banner, pointing out that rewards motivate students to get rewards, at the expense of any true interest in whatever it is that they are supposedly learning to do. Such rewards, they continue, do not prepare students to take responsibility for their own behavior—they only encourage mindless obedience. Teachers, they summarize, should avoid bribes and threats and instead try to create a caring community whose members solve problems collaboratively and decide together how they want their classroom to function.

> "You cannot teach a man anything; you can only help him find it within himself."
> — Galileo

> "Self-education is, I firmly believe, the only kind of education there is."
> — Isaac Asimov

> "Good teachers never teach anything. What they do is create the conditions under which learning takes place."
> —S.I. Hayakawa

Excellent points.

But a bit of clarification is needed. First, there's a real difference between a reward and a bribe. A reward makes you feel good about yourself; a bribe makes you feel like a sell-out. A spelling-bee trophy, for example, is a reward: it is a tangible emblem of your hard work and success. It's information. A teacher's assurance that "John is such a good boy because he's quiet in class," on the other hand, is a bribe: intangible proof that John has traded his individuality, dignity, and humanity for demeaning praise (remember Albert/Taz?).

Second, I argue that dogs and humans share an amazingly oxymoronic quality. We are both simultaneously social and competitive creatures: social creatures who realize that teamwork is the best way to get a job done, yet competitive creatures who want to be as high on the social ladder as possible. This is how so many of us can simultaneously support the notions that all human beings are equal but that the (fill in the nationality) are the best people in the world. This is how Amish farmers can get together in teams to raise a barn while competing against one another to see who can do their part of the job most quickly.

Historically, human social arrangements have attempted to address this paradox. In her book *The Second Stage*, Betty Friedan cites a number of studies conducted by Harvard University, Stanford Business School, West Point, and the Air Force Academy. The point of these studies was to determine just what is the best way to run a society. The researchers began by examining a variety of options, and came up with two basic—and fundamentally opposite—modes of human social organization: hierarchical and communal.

The hierarchical mode has historically dominated Western civilization. It is grounded on analytical, rational, quantitative thinking, and uses a hierarchically ordered relationship of authority. The power style is characterized as "direct", "aggressive," and highly competitive. Winning is everything; losing results in "a loss of face" (244). In educational terms, this is the stuff of lecture: the super Alpha is a kind of Moses, handing out scientific or aesthetic commandments left and right; the students compete to see who can follow them most closely. Answers are either "right" or "wrong."

This is precisely the sort of social arrangement Alfie Kohn distrusts, and with good reason. It might work for short-term projects which can be controlled by "order," but it's poorly equipped to deal with the sort of fluid change one hopes to find in a classroom. In the strictly hierarchical mode, one finds a tendency toward inflexibility — the researchers actually used the term "paralysis."

The social, communal paradigm is based upon synthesizing, intuitive, qualitative thinking; it uses a partnership model which employs a "contextual", "relational" power style. Its concern is communal growth and the quality of communal life, the sharing of internal resources and the establishment of interdependent adaptive relationships of mutual support. This is the type of classroom Alfie Kohn champions.

As do I.

But a strictly communal style is not without its own internal problems. Most of us have worked in touchy-feely communal groups where everyone was so determined to include everyone else and take all things into consideration that nothing was ever resolved; most of us have seen classrooms derailed by so much unfocussed "class participation" that nothing was ever learned.

Humans will never shake off their competitive nature, nor will they ever be willing to sacrifice their sociability. The best model for social and/or educational progress will have to make room for both aspects of the human (and canine) psyche: it's a matter of an almost Zen-like balance. Weight either side too heavily and the structure may collapse.

Third, whether we like it or not, reward is a fundamental basis of our culture. It's certainly the essence of Judeo-Christian religion: follow God's Ten Commandment rubric and you get a "Pass" and go to heaven; screw up and you get a "Fail" and go to hell. The legal system is a combination of negative aversion (laws) and competition (trials); virtually all media deals with winners and losers, crime and punishment.

Fourth, by the time college teachers get hold of students, the poor kids have been pretty heavily indoctrinated — they're even in school *primarily* because it's expected of them — and many have a good deal of "natural" aversion to *all* things associated with college (except sports and sex — remember Plato?) I've found that I need to use reinforcement just to get them to the point where learning *can* be fun again.

And finally, as Kohn points out, "teachers operate within significant constraints" (159). Many teachers loathe grades — I certainly do. My relationship with my class changes significantly when the first set of exams are handed back — no matter how hard I've tried to downplay the assessment, they still perceive themselves as having be relegated to a status designated by their grade.

But the kids aren't the only ones who have been indoctrinated: so have college administration officers and Promotion and Tenure committees. Whether teachers like it or not, our professional assessments and advancement are directly linked to our grading policies in the classroom. A wonderful professor I know has been doing competence-based grading for years. Her kids turn out wonderful, thoughtful, highly creative work, and adore her. But because her final grades are, according to her Promotion and Tenure committee, "too high," and because they are based on "qualitative rather than quantitative assessment," she'll languish as an Assistant Professor until the day she retires. Alfie Kohn is a brilliant psychologist, and a gifted and persuasive thinker and writer, but he's never undergone the peculiar brutalities of the tenure and promotion system. Perhaps that's why he sounds so nice and sane.

But Alfie Kohn and his champions certainly do make valid points.

We can't follow our students through life, handing them quarters. Heck, we can't even follow them through their four-year college experience. Even if we could, we wouldn't: who wants to teach someone to work purely for what others give them? I wouldn't do that to, well, a dog.

At some point, both dogs and human must move past conditioned reinforcement to self-reinforcement: performing tasks—indeed, creating tasks—for the sheer joy of accomplishment.

Hence, Part II of this book.

Part II
Self-Reinforcement

"The aim of education is, or should be, to teach people to educate themselves."
—Arnold J. Toynbee

"A teacher is one who makes himself progressively unnecessary."
— Thomas Caruthers

"To me education is a leading out of what is already there in the pupil's soul."
—Muriel Sparks.

"Education is a private matter between the person and the world of knowledge and experience, and has little to do with school or college."
- Lillian Smith

5

Prey Drive and Competition

> "It's a dog-eat-dog world, and I'm wearing
> Milk Bone shorts."
>
> —Kelly Allen

B oth dogs and humans are natural hunters. The urge to kill is hardwired into our psyches—we do not have many ancestors who did not enjoy the hunt, since they were unlikely to eat, and thus didn't last long enough to make it into the gene pool. Today, however, most of us—both canine and human— have transferred this primal urge into more socially acceptable outlets.

Example: consider the picture at the beginning of this section. Even those of us relatively unfamiliar with the canine psyche realize that the natural prey of a Parson Russell Terrier is probably not a stuffed toy duck. Yet since Hobbes (so called because he's nasty, brutish, and short) is not permitted to terrorize the local cat, squirrel, and pigeon populations, he must make do with what he has.

As must humans. Some people actually do hunt real animals—I live in rural Pennsylvania ("out where God lost His shoes" according to my husband), and the annual onslaught of city dwellers hell-bent on killing a rural deer makes the locals hide everything from their cows to their llamas throughout the season.

Other would-be human predators shoot golf instead of deer. More sedentary types exercise their predatory urges vicariously: watching football games, for example, and cheering when the defense chases down and brings a quarterback to earth (Mike Ditka didn't call Doug Flutie "Bambi" for nothing).

Non-violent types—such as I—satisfy themselves by non-violent means: solving crosswords, for example, or Sudoko puzzles (listen for the satisfied "Yesss" when the solver enters the final letter or number). Academics relish the "Aha!" moment when we "kill" the problem: finally figuring out exactly what the thesis of the damned essay we're reviewing *is*, or the relief we feel when the publisher actually accepts the manuscript (pending revisions, of course).

All of this is the same for students as well, of course. Awash in energy and hormones, they're even more prey-driven than adults are. Try this experiment: the next time you're addressing a class: get out from behind the lectern, or out of your seat—whatever— and *present a moving target as you speak*. Move up and back; crowd students' personal space for an instant then walk away. Walk to the rear of the class as you're speaking. Pace. Move your arms.

Your students—any audience, for that matter—*won't be able to take their eyes off you*. They can't. They're hard-wired by centuries of prey drive not to. On the outside, they're semi-civilized college students or perhaps even colleagues; on the inside, they're predators, absolutely fascinated by motion and activity. Good little wolves.

"There are young people out there cutting raw cocaine with chemicals from the local hardware store. They are manufacturing new highs and new products by soaking marijuana in ever changing agents, and each of these new drugs is more addictive, more deadly and less costly than the last. How is it that we have failed to tap that ingenuity, that sense of experimentation? How is it that these kids who can measure grams and kilos and can figure out complex monetary transactions cannot pass a simple math or chemistry test?"

—Senator Herb Kohl, from the U.S. Senate Hearing, "Crisis in Math and Science Education."

Prey drive is one of the single most valuable tools in a teacher's arsenal. But many teachers don't seem to realize that it can be useful—or even relevant—to good teaching. Or if they do, they certainly make no use of its power. Think of it. How many times have you heard colleagues complain that, thanks to television and film, students today have no long-term attention spans? That the generation reared on *Sesame Street* expects their education to come in thirty-second multimedia sound bites! That they have no perseverance! No determination!! and no willingness to meet and grapple with a problem!!!

Riiiiight. (You know, English could use a good irony marker.)

Excuse me, but these are the same students who will spend hours — sometimes days — engrossed in a computer video game. They will devise incredibly creative and complicated ways to solve a complex web of problems. "Oh, geez — how did I miss that one? You have to put the silver marble *in your mouth* before you cross the Bridge of Death!" (the mom in me shudders to think where *else* they inserted the silver marble before coming up with this "obvious" solution). Then, not content with merely solving the obvious puzzle, they will continue on, seeking out and discovering "Easter eggs" — secret messages and images hidden by the game designer for only the best players to discover.

No long-term attention spans?
No perseverance?
No determination?
No willingness to meet and grapple with a problem?

As my collie colleague Folly would say, "Sheep-poop!"

Video games are wildly popular precisely because directly engage a part of the student psyche that is inherent in their hard-wired evolutionary base: their prey drive. And like any successful predator, students can be relentless in pursuit.

Take these supposedly unmotivated, unwilling young people, divide them into teams, give them a clear problem to solve, and offer the winners a prize they consider worth winning (my best team might be allowed to leave class fifteen minutes early — I figure they don't need the extra practice) and you will suddenly find yourself surrounded by intellectual athletes, flexing their brains, and hell-bent on victory.

Consider, for example, a typical remedial non-credit English class, and their less-than-enthusiastic attitude toward books in particular and libraries in general. Remedial classes are for the most part composed of highly bibliophobic students who approach the library sullenly, keeping their heads down for fear that their friends might see them go in. I spent over three years designing and reworking a prey-drive based library assignment that students would see as something other than pedagogical cruelty. Finally (with the help of some extremely creative teaching librarians), I've gotten it.

It's a sort of intellectual scavenger hunt, a game that uses the library as a playing field. Students work as teams to answer twenty to thirty questions ("What picture won the Oscar for Best Film of 1987? When did the word 'computer' enter the English language? Who won the Nobel Peace Prize in 1932? Who had the most RBIs in 2001? How many authors named 'Adams' are in our library collection?" and so forth...) within a set time limit. The students who get the most correct answers in the shortest period of time are the Grand Prize Winners.

The results are frankly amazing. Once the students realize that this is the bibliographic version of The Big Game, they set to work with Olympian zeal, sprinting through the stacks and often nearly taking out unwary library patrons who lack the grace and agility to get out of their way.

I suppose one of the most astounding—and gratifying—moments in my academic career was the spectacle of two of my least enthusiastic students giving one another noisy high-fives to celebrate discovering the biographical journal entry on Frank Zappa.

They won the competition, although I later discovered that they had come up with a revolutionary way to "cheat" during the game. They had actually gone so far as to sneak into the library the day before the hunt and draw a map of the place, marking specialized computers, microfilm sections, and reference holdings. In addition, they had even managed to discover a library "cheat sheet" hidden in plain sight (on the wall where patrons entered) that showed Library of Congress designations and the floors on which the appropriate books could be found. What a scam!

They had gotten their subversive mapping idea from—you guessed it—mapping the virtual rooms in video games.

After proudly accepting their "handsome gold trophies" (the Last of the Big Spenders, I sprang for Sacagawea gold-finished dollars on this exercise), one of the two even went so far as to award the project a particularly gushing accolade on his final class evaluation: "that stupid library thing wasn't really as dumb as I thought it would be."

Mini-Digression

I suppose that's my goal: making sure that the class is not quite as dumb as they thought it would be. I hope that they'll eventually come to believe that writing well—or even just coherently—is a skill that has some value. 105 is the class, after all, that no one wants to take—and most students are far more concerned with finding a scapegoat on whom to vent their embarrassment and frustration (that would be me—enter Darby, pursued by a gerund) than on learning how to write—indeed, they see any attempt to learn such skills as a tacit admission that they do indeed belong in a remedial class. I sidestep the aversion issue by taking a conspiratorial, rather than adversarial, position—no matter whose fault it is that they wound up here (poor high school preparation, unfeeling examiners, fate) my job is to get them out of a bad situation: they're drowning, and I'm the guy with the life preserver.

So I combine their instinct for self-preservation with some peer pressure. Toss in some *healthy* competition and add a pinch of status.

Competition can be cruel, especially when one cannot even imagine a vague possibility of not being a loser: take this from the person who was always chosen last in volleyball (and kickball, and softball, and basketball, and, and ...). The workshop, however, uses competition to provide models; it's a training camp designed to improve everyone's game. Its format does force students to compare their own essays with those of their classmates, and hierarchies of skill do emerge. Yet the function of competition here is not winning or losing, but making students realize that whether or not their notion that "all writing is unpleasant" is true, some writing is certainly more unpleasant than others.

I develop their taste, slowly, following my rubric and moving forward in small, completely manageable increments (heavily reinforcing each step, of course). I'll read a series of student titles aloud and ask the class to decide which accompanying paper they'd like to read first. None of them wants to produce the title that stands on the sidelines and gets chosen last (I shamelessly plug into sports idioms). And, since the production of a title is a relatively simple and manageable affair even for non-writers, they begin writing catchier, more successful ones—and in doing so, blunder into their first dim sense of reader awareness.

The process of competition (Go, Team! Go! Write, Team! Write!) continues through the opening sentence—again, a short and relatively manageable piece of prose (guess who won the "My prom was the most wonderful day of my life" versus "'CRASH! The glass shattered as my car rammed into the tree" title challenge). Then, buoyed by the double success of title and opening, we move on to the initial paragraph. Moving slowly, the class eventually produces entire essays that are entirely readable. The "good" writers in the class are not bored by the pace because they're busy trying to top their last effort—after all, they got a rep to maintain now—and helping the other members of their group. The weaker writers pick up

The Norton Anthology of Doggerel

Folly T. Dog, Ed.

speed by copying the style of their more wordly peers, mimicking prose technique just as an athlete copies a sports hero's golf or baseball swing.

By the end of the semester, peer pressure and competition have accomplished what I could never have hoped to: the students actually perceive effective writing as a means to achieve status.

Yet prey drive is only a relatively small part of your arsenal. You ain't seen nothin' yet!

6

Status and Pack Dynamics

"In Washington, it's dog eat dog. In academia, it's
exactly the opposite."
—-Robert Reich

L ike dogs and wolves, humans are social animals. A lone
wolf is a dead wolf—and he knows it. He must have the
stability of a pack in order to hunt, to procreate, and to rear
cubs. When people tell me they want a puppy "so it will bond with
me," I have to force back a smile. The dog you rescue from the
pound will probably bond with you within two or three days—or
whatever period of time it takes her to determine whether or not
yours is a transient or permanent home.[9] (More often than not, the
rescue dogs I have taken in take one look at my strong, well-
organized pack and settle into my home as if they'd been there for
years, and they will do *anything* to stay. A place for everyone, and
everyone ...)

---

[9] And we're talking a Velcro-dog, here: this poor dog has been out on the streets and is
incredibly grateful to have been adopted. A pup will just accept a home as its rightful due
and may very well flip you a dewclaw if asked to behave.

And, like dogs and wolves, human beings are hierarchical animals—and, given our 'druthers, we seek to be as high on the hierarchy as we can. I don't mean that we all want to be top dog— how many of us would *really* want to be President of the United States? Or Pope? Instead, we find the rank we are comfortable with and settle in.

Once we have it, we will fight fiercely to retain our status—just consider the words of Henry Kissinger, for example, who noted that, "University politics are vicious precisely because the stakes are so small."

Without a doubt, status is the most powerful human (and canine) motivator. It's even stronger than sex or food drives: a human will avoid sexual contact with lower status individuals, fearing that such contact will lower her own status; people will go hungry in order to have a thinner, higher status figure. Status is inextricably linked to tangible reward—a shiny BMW, designer clothes, a fashionable address.

It's also linked to competition and prey drive—the team/business/individual who "beats" the opposition, who "destroys" the opponent, is the higher status winner: the Top Dog.

Or, in dogspeak, the Alpha Dog.

6.1 The Alpha

Wolves and dogs (and, I will argue, humans) have a virtually identical status drive. Packs are ordered according to a strict hierarchy. Alpha wolves are the best of the best: the strongest, brightest, and most creative. They assume leadership and all the responsibilities that go along with it. They make the rules, and they give the orders.

Alphas are the wolves who take chances, learn, and make decisions. As a result of their superior physical and intellectual qualities, the pack functions effectively.

Alphas also enjoy the most rewards—the Alpha male and female are the only wolves who have sex; they eat first (and best), and are shown total deference by the other pack members.

Understandably, the Alphas are also the most stressed pack members. Responsibility is a double-edged sword.

6.2 The Beta

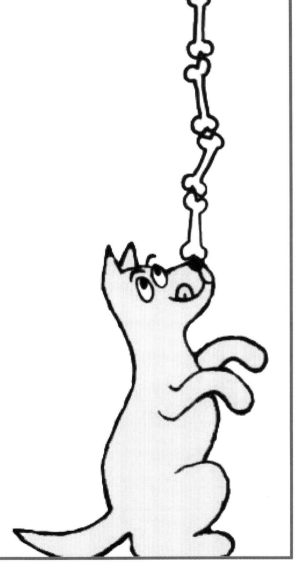

Betas, on the other hand, are first-rate followers and memorizers. They take direction well, obey rules faithfully (unless they're a high-level Beta-plus trying to move up and occupy what he perceives as a gap in the pack hierarchy), and avoid risks (again, unless they're upwardly mobile pups attempting a coup)—the perquisites of followers.

The Beta enjoys fewer rewards—no sex, lots of puppysitting, and a diet of leftovers—but the weight of the pack isn't on his withers.

6.3 The Omega

The remainder of the pack is arranged in descending order, Delta, Gammas, and so forth, all the way down to the Omega. Humans tend to feel sorry for this pack "goat," the one who receives no rewards other than pack membership—and is often attacked by other pack members just because they're in a bad mood.

But the Omega, too, has a place, a sense of belonging, and a function. He basks in the reflected glory of his loftier pack members—like the water boy on a football team. And, like the water boy, the Omega is an essential part of pack balance, just as important as an Alpha; if he is somehow lost, another pack member will take his place. He is, like the Alpha, a boundary marker; his presence defines the limits of the pack.

His rewards are few, but so are his responsibilities. He has the very last choice of food, yet he does have something to eat—the pack will see to that, even if they're starving.

Do these arrangements sound at all familiar? They should. In any gathering of humans, it's fairly easy to spot the Alphas, the Betas and other middlers, and—of course—the Omegas.

Academia is certainly no exception: two members of the Physics department, jostling for position. One will be Alpha, the other won't. Guess the status of the housekeepers in the dorms, virtually ignored by students, administration, and faculty alike.

And don't forget the rest of us: everyone in between!

"The mediocre teacher tells. The good teacher explains. The superior teacher demonstrates. The great teacher inspires. "

—William Arthur Ward

"School is a building that has four walls—with tomorrow inside."

—Lon Watters

7

Bringing out the Alpha in Your Students

Grrr.

S urprisingly—or maybe it's not so surprising—traditional education works along the same rules that we associate with pack dynamics.

Consider the typical lecture class. In pack terms, it looks something like this:

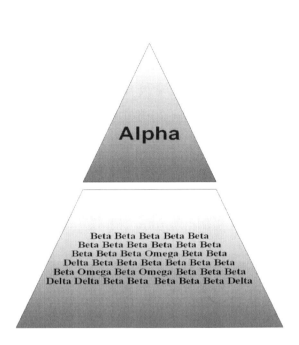

The lecture mode has lasted for centuries because—in its own peculiar fashion—it's comfortable for everyone. Order is consistently maintained; like good little wolves, no student (except an exceptionally courageous Alpha wannabe) ever defies the professors. It's a model highly effective for transmitting supposed "facts." Example: if I assert in a lecture that Shelley's "Hymn to Intellectual Beauty" is his best poem—because I heard that "fact" in a lecture during my undergraduate career—hundreds of pens will note the second-hand opinion as spoken truth, and future generations of lecturers will pass it on *ad nauseum*. Hence, the model tends to produce stasis. It rewards followers, memorizers, risk-avoiders—hmmm, where have I heard this before?—and tends to penalize radicalism and creativity. It is directed not toward the production of new Alphas, but to the comfort of all.

So what's wrong with a little comfort?

Nothing.   Except that as educators, we'd like to produce innovators, risk takers, creative thinkers: Alphas. Well, at least *I'd* like to. And if you've read this far, you'd probably like to, too.

Let's look at two sample wolfy/doggy packs and I'll show you what I mean.

1. A peaceful pack.

I have five Border Collies. I also like to have peace in my home. Thus, I live *la vida* lecture, and follow a strict pack hierarchy. My Alpha dog Folly eats first, goes out the door first, and gets in the car first. She goes to work with me every day while the other dogs

stay home. The rest of the pack is fed, trained, exercised, and so forth in pack hierarchical order. Everyone knows where he or she stands, and everyone is comfortable. I have no dog fights.

Problem is, I have only one Alpha—only one dog mentally and psychologically fit to withstand the intellectual rigors of a four-day dog show; of airplane, bus, and train travel; of lodgings in strange places; and of educational workshops. When she retires—when another, younger, stronger dog moves up and takes her place—I will have a different single Alpha. *But I can have only one at a time.* If I had two or more Alphas, they would constantly be duking it out in order to prove exactly who was truly running things.

2. A winning pack.

I have a friend who, like me, has five Border Collies. Because she is a nationally ranked dog show competitor, however, she needs to have five dogs who are mentally and psychologically fit to withstand most of the aforementioned rigors: four-day dog shows; airplane, bus, and train travel; lodgings in strange places.

For this she needs five Alphas, so she feeds a different dog first each day, lets a different dog enter the car first each time she goes for a drive, gives treats in varying order. She has many, many trophies, ribbons, awards and honors. She also has many, many dog fights. Her home can be an uncomfortable place to be around (it could make you absolutely long for a squabble as simple as "Mom! Kayla's *look*ing at me!"). But boy, does she have great working dogs. And even the weakest of her multiple Alphas is probably much stronger than my lone one—after all, there is no complacency in her house, since each dog is constantly striving to be the best.

> "'Do you think you can maintain discipline?' asked the Superintendent. 'Of course I can,' replied Stuart. 'I'll make the work interesting and the discipline will take care of itself.'"
>
> — E.B. White, *Stuart Little*

Face it: when there are multiple thinkers and innovators in the same room—when true learning is taking place among a wide variety of interpretation—academia (hey, *all* disciplines) can be a very uncomfortable place.

Perhaps learning *should* be an uncomfortable process—I always knew that I was *really* learning when my head seemed to hurt from the huge ideas crammed inside. My classrooms seem to be most exciting when students challenge one another—when they challenge me—when things are not a matter of taking down notes but of solving (and frequently causing) problems.

If this kind of near anarchy frightens you—if you enjoy the peace and quiet that accompanies a lecture class chock-full of Betas,

Deltas Gammas, and so forth, then read no further—heck, you've probably already read way too far.

But if you want the excitement and danger of a multiple Alpha classroom, read on.

Look at it this way. You don't have to *live* with them—you just have to deal with them for a couple of hours a week.

"Yeah, we're all Alphas. Who exactly wants to know?

And *why*?"

8

Multiple Alphas in the Classroom

T he first step in developing multiple Alphas is to find the potential Alphas you've already got. With dogs, it's fairly easy. The Alpha dog always takes the bone away from the other dogs. The Alpha invariably wins any tug-of war contests with other adult dogs. The Alpha will generally receive the most attention from the other dogs. The Alpha will win all stare-downs with the other dogs. The Alpha becomes jealous if the other dogs receive attention from the owner. The Alpha expects the best, eats first, and takes the best sleeping area, whether directly next to the owner or far away in a corner.

Alpha students can be more subtle—they're the cleverest of the bunch, after all, but are ultimately just as readily identified.

Give a group of four students a figurative bone, in the form of what I call a "speaking pen." Explain that only the student holding the pen is allowed to speak: the others must listen until the speaker relinquishes it—ostensibly, this process will prevent everyone from speaking at once. The student who seizes the pen first is probably your Alpha.

There are other signs as well. She'll win student debates. He'll easily gain and hold the attention of other students. If you keep an eye on student eye contact and body language, you'll notice the ones with the steady gaze and aggressive body position: the Alphas. The student who is the "ham," who must have your attention in and out of the classroom, who adores being treated as your peer—probably an Alpha, but only if she can ham it up and still retain peer respect. The students who take the choice seating as their right—either the first row far left, or far right; or the last row rear center—again, likely Alphas.

> "The principal goal of education is to create men who are capable of doing new things, not simply of repeating what other generations have done—men who are creative, inventive and discoverers."
>
> —Jean Piaget

Let's assume you've found three or four obvious Alphas in a class of say, twenty-five. You'd like more.

How do you multiply them? By shuffling and re-shuffling your "pack" of students, just as I shuffle and re-shuffle litters of puppies when they arrive in my home.

When I have a litter of new pups, I don't want cozy comfort. Since virtually all of my puppies are sold as competition or working dogs (hey, *I* won't have to live with them), *i.e.*, dogs who need to be capable of independent thought in order to function as a full member of the human/canine team, *I want to be able to develop as many Alphas as possible.*

I begin by identifying the baby Alphas—a fairly easy task. They're the first to walk, the first to bark (okay, the first to "bark"), and the first to shove their brothers and sisters away from the food source. I break up the litter into groups of two to four, depending on the number of pups I have (if there are multiple litters, I'll mix them up). I put the most aggressive pups in one group, and let them duke it out—they'll learn manners and mutual respect. More importantly, however, I'll separate the second group of less aggressive pups and let them work out a hierarchy for themselves. Inevitably, an Alpha will emerge—it must: nature abhors a vacuum. Wolves and dogs (and humans) are genetically hard-wired to produce a leader—they would be unable to survive, otherwise. To mix a metaphor, I get a big fish—in a *very* small pond, perhaps, but a big fish nonetheless.

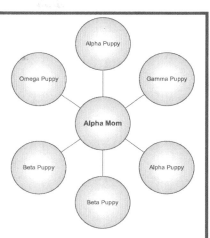

The original litter probably looked something like the one above when they were whelped (rather like a classroom of students on the first day, with the teacher functioning as Alpha Mom).

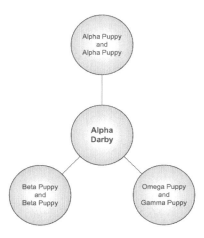

Very cute, and left to themselves, the pups will develop a hierarchy leading to comfort and pack stasis. And only one very bossy Alpha puppy running things, which I don't want. When they're weaned, however, I begin shuffling the litter, and my new improved multiple Alpha model looks like the one on the left (rather like my students after I've broken them into multiple Alpha-based workshop groups).

In the first case Mom is the Alpha, overseeing things; in the second case, it's me, the observer/ trainer/ teacher.

When my new Alphas develop in the less aggressive packs, I'll shift things around again—and again—until virtually every puppy has had a shot at the Alpha experience. Some of them won't take to it—they're natural Betas, Deltas, or Omegas and are happy that way and will never change. They'll make wonderful pets. But everyone will have had at least a shot at being the leader, the innovator, the play instigator, the creative thinker, the puppy on top of the pile.

These mini-Alphas are noisy, confrontational puppies, who would be totally out of place in a traditional wolf pack, which encourages hierarchy and peace. Many blood-curdling soprano puppy snarls emanate from my canine nursery; hundreds of puppy tussles occur as the order of things is sorted and resorted. It's not comfortable, but it's not dangerous: as with students, most of the jockeying for position is a matter of posturing— extended sessions of growly-face  games and non-lethal wrestling matches. And it's a highly effective way to produce multiple top-working Alpha dogs from a small population.

These arrangements may sound oddly familiar to those of you who use peer learning methods. When educators shift away from the lecture/hierarchical pack mode into smaller peer-run groups, the classroom moves from an orderly, monovocal place to a messy polyvocal area. Sometimes it looks like chaos. But it is an area in which students (like the puppies) are challenged, self-motivated, and excited about what they're doing. It's a space that encourages critical thinking and original ideas. It may be uncomfortable at times—indeed, in many of my classes I feel more like a referee than a teacher—but it's productive.

Here's how the classroom model that I call "Alpha Squares" looks like in a class of twenty-four students:

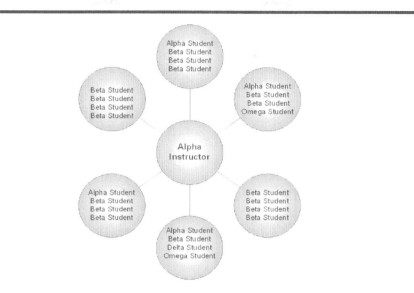

If you employ the peer-learning format, this might well resemble your own class at the beginning of the semester: teams of students, grouped to accommodate individual strengths and weaknesses. I used this model effectively for years.

I made one small mistake, however.

Okay. It was one *critical* mistake.

My students were so comfortable in the "packs" that they complained noisily when I suggested they shuffle themselves into different groups. They enjoyed stasis; they were comfortable. I enjoy comfort, too, so I didn't fight them; I let them stay in their stable groups for the entire semester, congratulating myself on my ability to instill such high levels of "team spirit" in my students. In short, I had turned them into human versions of my pack at home: peaceful, well-organized, with a single Alpha.

Wrong move. Yes, their group was a team, but, more importantly, it was a *pack*.

They had established their own hierarchies; like wolves, each person knew his or her place in the order of things. Oh, I wound up with more Alphas than I would have in a traditional lecture format—in a class of twenty-four, I had six instead of none.

But when I finally began to follow my own puppy-rearing methods—shifting the Alpha pattern throughout the semester, and constantly watching for emerging Alphas—I wound up with twelve or fifteen! Yes, I had up to fifteen Alphas to watch and manage, and a lot more student confrontation to deal with, but I also had many more active scholars and many fewer passive memorizers.

Reshuffling the "pack" on a regular basis allows individual strengths to emerge, and provides the opportunity for each student to get a taste of Alpha-hood. As is the case with my pups, some of them won't take to it—they're natural Betas, Deltas, or Omegas, and are happy that way—they will never change. They'll make wonderful followers. But everyone will at least have had a shot at being the leader, the innovator, the instigator, the creative thinker. Some will find it to be an acquired taste.

But back to my litter. When my puppies are older, I employ another Alpha development strategy. When the litter is happily playing in an outdoor dog run, I'll go in and select a single pup, remove it, and play with it just outside the run. There will be lots of treats, lots of praise, lots of fun.

And lots of envy, since the entire production is presented directly in front of the other pups. Everyone gets a turn, and each pup revels in being the center of not only my attention, but the attention of the rest of the pack as well. It's good to be Alpha, they learn. I call my classroom version of this strategy the "Alpha Circle." It's adapted from Kathleen Galvin's "Minute Round" and looks something like this:

In this model, the students and professor are seated in a circle. All traditional academic hierarchies are—at least on the surface—broken down; we're all Alphas together, in a simultaneously confrontational and non-confrontational setting. I might pick a student to begin, or allow individual students to volunteer (students learn quickly that going first is a decided advantage, since by doing so they will prevent anyone else from using "their" idea—see below), or I might choose a student at random.

Each participant has one minute—no more, no less—to discuss the

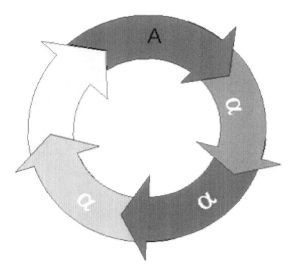

reading, the problem—whatever the material is that will be handled that day. Strict wolfy rules are followed: the one-minute-Alpha must be shown respect by the remainder of the "pack": listeners must listen attentively—no sidebar conversations, no perusals of other classwork. They must meet the speaker's eyes unless she specifically directs them to a page in the text.

The speaker, in turn, must act like a proper Alpha: although he might be tempted to stare fixedly at the teacher, with a deer-in-the-headlights terrified-prey stare, he must shift his gaze around the circle so as to include everyone. (Some students simply cannot look away from the professor; in that case I move outside the circle and sit out of their line of sight.) The only exception to the "eye" rule is made in the case of students with extremely high levels of stage fright,[10] who may read previously prepared material to defuse their anxiety. The Alpha role thus shifts, quite literally, from minute to minute.

Initially, stress and resistance is quite high, but over time most students overcome their reservations. The interminable sixty seconds ("*No one* can talk that long!") shrinks to a marginally sufficient length ("Hey! I had more to say!").

Most students come to enjoy the exercise; a few (usually diehard Deltas and Omegas) loathe it unremittingly. Interestingly, on the school's end-of-semester student evaluations, the Alpha Circle is always listed on both the "Part of Class Most Liked" and "Part of Class Most Disliked" sections—sometimes even on a single evaluation. Go figure.

An Aside on End-of-semester Evaluations

Rather than find out what the students think of the class when it's too late to change things (remember punishment?), I employ short, informal mid-semester class evaluations. I ask two questions, to be answered anonymously: 1) what would you keep about this class? and 2) what would you change? If the "change" responses are widespread and reasonable (sample: "WAY too much reading and we never look at half of the assigned material in class"), I'll change things in midstream. The class will then come to realize that their input is valued (mutual respect), and I wind up teaching more effectively to a specific classroom population.

---

[10] A study was done a few years ago, in which people were asked what they feared most in their lives. Death came in second. Public speaking was the clear winner.

Meanwhile, back at the Minute Round

With more advanced students, I'll allow what I call "tag-team" rounds: if one student's presentation touches off an idea in another, the circle can be disrupted momentarily. When the second student has finished her comment, we return to the original (reassuring) order. (And commenting students are still responsible for their minute when the circle comes around to them.)

Of course, some students come to class unprepared. They were ill; they broke up with a girlfriend/boyfriend. Okay; no problem. I permit each student one "pass" per semester, more in extreme cases when they've cleared it with me ahead of time. (I'm certainly not out to punish students caught in difficulties.)

But without a pass, the student must still spend a minute speaking: he can explain why he's unprepared, or what he did instead of preparing, or what he had for breakfast, or the plot of a recent movie he's seen—any topic at all. But he must fill out the entire minute.

It's an agonizing process for the individual, but the remainder of the group looks on with all the smug enjoyment of a wolf pack watching a lame moose flounder in heavy snow. I have never yet had a student screw up more than twice—as one young man confessed to me, "I do the reading now because I don't want to look like a jerk." He doesn't blame me for his predicament, nor does he look to me for positive or negative response.

This is important: I am careful to give no punishment to the unprepared; there's nothing they can do about their situation at this point. Instead, I smile encouragingly and sympathetically as the poor schm... I mean as the student struggles through the hour-long minute. This is negative reinforcement at its most effective:

students realize that it was *their* choice to gain or lose status by appearing as a dazzler or a doofus; next time they're self-motivated to prepare.

In larger classes, where such a round would be impossible due to sheer numbers (there are only so many "minutes" in an academic hour, after all, and I'd like to devote some time to directed discussion or group work), I'll "deal" ten student names at random. In a large class, I will have assigned each student a playing card at the beginning of the semester. Then I'll shuffle my matching deck and "deal" the student participants at the beginning of each class. Any given student could thus possibly be expected to participate several times in a row. They know the fix isn't in—I clearly lack both the mental and physical coordination required of a card sharp—and thus everyone must be prepared. And they *are* prepared: the prospect of "looking like a jerk" in front of a tremendous number of their peers absolutely horrifies them. As it would certainly horrify you or me.

And so the semester progresses, with students gradually acquiring confidence along the way.

As the course winds down, however, I return them to the lecture mode—after all, in the "real world," they'll probably be leading meetings, doing presentations, and accepting awards—Alphas tend to do things like that.

So here's the final model of Alpha development, which I call the "Leader of the Pack":

Look familiar?

Well, it should.

It is, of course, the horrible traditional end-of-semester gee-we-hate-this oral presentation that we have all come to know and abominate — but with a difference.

No longer will it be the quintessence of fear and loathing unto finals.

Those of you who have been teaching a while will be sure to envision the

```
     Alpha
  for ten minutes

      Alphas
(impatient for their turn)
Assorted Betas, Gammas,
     Deltas and
      Omegas

       me
```

traditional scene: the droning, robotic student, frozen by terror, reading a paper that no one listens to; the yawning, bored listeners, some asleep, some doing their fill-in-the-subject-as-long-as-it-isn't-the-one-in-progress homework, some checking the polish on their nails intently; the professor, wondering if the nineteen years spent in school was supposed to lead to this, and thinking how nice it would be to open a quiet little used bookstore that serves latte — make that a lovely *bon vin blanc*...

Introduce multiple Alphas into the equation, however, and these "traditional" presentations are anything but.

First, the presenter's stress level is significantly lower than it would be had the class been run in lecture mode: the student is used to speaking up—and out. These students have enjoyed a semester's worth of successful trial Alpha runs with squares and circles: they have the voice of their status.

Second, I cheat. I grade the oral presentation on a bifurcated scale: half the grade is based on the quality of information presented, the remaining half on sheer entertainment value. Thus the highest grade a student who reads a great paper but loses the class's attention can possibly expect would be a "C": an "A" for information and an "F" for entertainment.

The lowered stress level and the semester-long emphasis on creative, innovative Alpha thinking really kicks in at this point: indeed, I have had students from other classes crowd in just to see the show. Balloons explode, PowerPoint animations dance, multimedia effects surround us. One literature student even did a presentation on John Keats' "Lamia"—a poem about a young woman who has been turned into a gorgeously colored serpent— with a four-foot gorgeously colored serpent draped around her neck.

The Alpha student—confident (perhaps even cocky), inventive, and enthusiastic, is in her element: at the head of the pack, with all eyes glued on the leader.

Part III
The Classroom:
a Survivor's Guide

Feeling lucky,
teach?
Go ahead:
make my day.

9
Armageddon 101

Using Canine Pack Dynamics to Deal with the Disruptive Student

We've all experienced it. A class we teach one year with no problems at all turns ugly the next—and we're using exactly the same text and approaches. What happened? Or a student we perceive as an angel is considered a troublemaker by our colleagues (or, even worse, they'll see what we consider our class fiend as a hard-working, earnest scholar). What makes a good class (or good student) go bad?

First, I suppose, we need to determine what makes a "bad" class—or student. Disruption, I suppose, in all its myriad shapes and sizes.

The war stories are endless. There are the passive disrupters: gum poppers, note passers, whisperers, hair brushers, manicurists, sleepers, text messagers, telephoners—and telephone answerers. One of my colleagues had a young man in his class who would show up every day with a full lunch—greasy cheeseburger, large fries, and a milk shake. He'd unwrap the meal and noisily chomp his way through class. And then belch loudly. Another had a young woman who engaged in various types of bizarre behavior. Example: one day during a lecture on Plato's *Republic*, she yawned, extracted cotton balls and a large bottle of alcohol from her backpack, pulled up her blouse, and proceeded to clean her newly inserted navel ring.

And, when things get *really* bad, there might be active disruption: almost every teacher I've met has at one time or another been forced to deal with interruptions, confrontations, obscenity, racist, sexist or homophobic language, insults—sometimes even physical threats.

There are, of course, many theories as to why individual students are disruptive. Rudolf Dreikurs identifies four causes: a student might feel a need for attention and use misbehavior to get it—and in the process become a class "star" without academic effort. Or disruption might be a threatened Alpha's way to indicate the lack of the class' value to him—he's not incapable; the class is not worthy of his time. Some students are what Dreikurs calls "Power Seekers:" a student who doesn't trust the teacher as a leader senses a power gap needing to be filled. Or, there are the "Revengers" who tend to feel inadequate; instead of blaming themselves, however, they turn into "injustice collectors" who blame their teachers. "Failure avoiders" are generally students with high levels of natural aversion who feel doomed and fear failure and peer ridicule.

To Dreikurs' list I would add cultural differences (some male students reared in highly patriarchal societies might find it difficult to defer to a woman in authority, for example), psychological problems (not uncommon in schools with open enrollment policies), and boredom. In the first two cases I would suggest getting outside help (a faculty member of a similar cultural background can explain things to the student much more easily than the professor under attack; a psychologist can assess the magnitude of the student's difficulties and perhaps offer her coping strategies).

Extreme student boredom, however—extreme enough to cause disruption—is generally an issue exclusive to very dull lecture classes. If a teacher must lecture, she must either learn to deal with student ennui or become an entertaining (*i.e.,* a comical or galvanizing) lecturer.

I would argue, however, that in almost every case the central reason behind almost all class disruption is professor- rather than student-based. *Class disruption occurs when there is a perceived lack of leadership.* As Dreikurs himself notes, disruption is a result of the student's "mistaken assumption about the way he can find a place and gain status" (Dreikurs, 36). Yup, pack behavior and status once again.

So, let's say you've lost the class. Or, worse, you never had it in the first place. How do you assume leadership?

The answer is (once again) the careful use of pack dynamics and status. If the class does get out of hand, it is probably a combination of lack of assertiveness on your part, plus a failure to watch your students carefully. You can tell from their body language if students are insecure, uncomfortable, angry, or confused. More importantly, you can use canine/lupine models to prevent class disruption from ever rearing its ugly head in the first place.

Note...

Some teachers do not need to consider such things as student misbehavior. They are "natural" Alphas—they're the ones who don't need to read this book—indeed, who would consider a topic such as student disruption a *non sequitur*. They will never be challenged in a classroom because student respect is their perquisite. Those of you who fall into such a category may feel free to ignore the following sections.

Such educators enjoy a "natural" Alpha status which may be the result of fame—perhaps they're Nobel or Pulitzer Prize winners, or pundits seen on television, or authors of highly successful publications. Think Henry Kissinger or Albert Einstein. Or they might just have powerful charisma or just be extremely likeable. Think Arnold Schwarzenegger or Mr. Rogers.

But what about the rest of us? Think Barney Fife. Where do *we* begin? And how?

"I'm [Absolutely Not] Ready for my Close-up, Mr. De Mille"

I *know* you're not going to want to hear this, but the first step in becoming an Alpha is videotape—indeed, it's useful to go through the videotaping process even if you're not having any problems with your class. Every one of us—even "natural" Alphas—can improve our teaching, and videotape is a powerful tool which helps us do so. Have your audio visual people or a student Mass Communications major tape your class—or even better, tape several of your classes.

If that sounds too painful and public, borrow a camcorder and tripod from the audio visual people, set it up in the rear of the room and tape yourself. Then watch the result in the privacy of your own home with the drapes pulled and the lights out. Have a glass of wine (or scotch) at the ready.

Watch the videotape at least twice (I'm assuming the first viewing will be too much of a shock to permit you any sort of self-critique — always is for me). But watch it again. You're a critical thinker, after all, accustomed to analysis. You'll know exactly how to discriminate between effective and ineffective teaching.

No? Well, here's what to look for.

9.1 Voice

A ctually, your initial analytical approach to the videotape won't involve *looking* at all. Instead, you'll *listen* to yourself.

Do you sound like an Alpha? Or like a dying rabbit? Is your voice powerful, low, clear, and inflected? Or is it weak, squeaky, whiny, and monotonal?

Remember that your **tone of voice** provides an almost infinite reflection of your emotion, meaning, and mood. Consider a single word such as "Yes": it can be sarcastic, superior, submissive, or …

Pitch also sends powerful messages: a wolf will bark or growl in order to assert dominance, but whine when he is being submissive: "Hey, listen to me! I'm prey; I won't hurt you; please don't hurt me." Think about it. What happens to the pitch of your voice when you're speaking to a baby? It tends to go up, since you want the baby to consider you harmless. Growl at the poor kid and he'll probably burst into tears (and his parents probably won't be inviting you to their house again soon).

In a classroom marked by disruption, you want to sound like predator, not prey. Think of Darth Vader as a shrill soprano. Would he be quite as intimidating without James Earl Jones' *basso profundo*? Probably not. That's because humans, like their lupine counterparts, have learned over the eons to take a low, predatory voice *very* seriously. (The ones who didn't would not have survived long enough to enter the gene pool.)

Therefore, when you are attempting to assert control without resorting to direct confrontation (which is always a mistake—I'll discuss this later), try to lower the pitch of your voice as much as you can and still be comfortable—remember that prey squeaks, and that a low voice signals power. Strident speech marks desperation.

Remember also that the vocal chords are constructed so that the lowest tones are produced when they're fully relaxed—that's why people's voices tend to rise in pitch when they're excited or afraid. In the privacy of your home or office, practice speaking in situations that might make you nervous: difficult verbal acts such as asking a favor, disciplining a student, telling a student that he's failing the class, for example, or refusing an extension on a paper. Your voice might seem harsh and raspy, so try to even it out: practice until you can do so in a low, relaxed voice.

There's more to voice control than tone, however. Pay attention to your **pacing** as well. Too rapid speech can signal nervousness or anxiety. Too slow, and your class drops out (although sometimes a few moments at a slower pace can be useful—when you wish to emphasize an important idea, for example). You also need to determine your voice quality: don't whine or you'll sound either weak or manipulative. And for heaven's sake speak up—and out.

Now go back and look at the tape again. You've lowered your voice and adjusted you pace. You've practiced difficult vocal situations and now sound like an Alpha.

But of course, there's more to do. Do you look and act like an Alpha?

9.2 A Teacher in Wolf's Clothing

"Beowulf put on his warrior's dress, and had no fear for his life. His war-shirt, hand-fashioned, broad and well-worked, was . . . to cover his body-cave so that foe's grip might not harm his heart, or grasp of angry enemy his life."

—Beowulf

Wolves don't wear clothes, of course, but Alphas of any species tend to be extremely careful about their grooming. Your clothing makes a statement about you even before you introduce yourself to the class. So consider carefully how you dress. Is your clothing fairly conservative? It should be, especially if you're a young teacher (or look like one).

The "power suit" earned its name; a hangover from Beowulf's eighth-century war-suit, its pin-striped conventionality is designed to downplay the emotionalism associated with personal identity, and its shoulder-padded, slim matching pants/skirt silhouette highlights upper-body strength. Its "broad and well-worked" design translates into careful tailoring because careful tailoring—rightly or wrongly—suggests high status and power.

Hey (or "Yo"). You might look great in trendy, colorful, youth-oriented clothes, but you'll also look young enough to preclude being taken seriously as an Alpha (and of course, if you're far too old to wear teenagers' clothes, you'll be an anachronistic figure of fun). Yes, it's very true that some ultra-Alpha professors can wear T-shirts and jeans and still command respect. Hell, they could probably wear a Bozo the Clown suit—complete with red nose—and *still* command respect. No, it's *not* fair. But when a teacher is struggling with a difficult class, youthful garb is simply not an option.

Indeed, even well-cut suits may not be enough. Good clothes must be cared for. Do your clothes fit well? Too loose clothes signal someone down on her luck; too tight clothes suggest someone who's in denial about his weight.

Is your clothing baggy or in poor condition? Are your shoes beat up with worn heels? Students size up everything about you the first time you walk into a classroom.[11] Even colors make a tremendous difference—if you're having trouble establishing

---

[11] Early in my career, I was lecturing on the poet Robert Browning, and when I began to discuss his take on the "eternal moment," a student who had up until then effectively tuned out of the class suddenly grew alert and focused. Convinced that I had finally reached her, my lecturing suddenly became more and more energetic, and she became more and more "into" the lecture. At the end of the class, she approached me (as I had instinctively known she would), looked at me with deep intensity, and asked, "Is that a perm?" Just one more reason why I no longer lecture.

yourself as an Alpha, go for navy, which is generally perceived as "weightier" and more "serious" than lighter colors. Tans and grays for men, and pinks and yellows for women, for example, are perceived as light, "fluffy" "emotional" colors. Alphas want to project substance and power. Men looking for a bit more Alpha *gravitas* should drift toward black and navy; women wishing to be taken a bit more seriously should limit themselves to black, brown to camel, burgundy, blue to navy, beige to taupe, and all shades of gray.

If you're old enough to remember it, think of the first Kennedy-Nixon debate in 1960. Richard Nixon was pale and sweating, his shirt collar loose on his neck from a recent illness — and he wore a light gray suit that made him seem

> …insubstantial and meek. On black and white television, he and the backdrop were the same color, a combination of wet cement and cardboard. He became invisible but for a pair of rubbery hands wiping sweat on his ashen face with a white hankie (Robert Sherrill).

Interestingly enough, people who listened to the debate on the radio thought Nixon had won. Those who watched it on television considered Kennedy the clear winner.

Clothes may not completely make the Alpha, but they certainly *help*.

Micro-addenda

There's an added benefit to well-tailored, conservative clothing. It will favorably impress your teaching colleagues and the administration — handy when promotion and tenure decisions come around.

9.3 Posture

A nother powerful nonverbal tool that projects power and confidence is the way in which you carry yourself. Do you stand erect and relaxed, leaning slightly forward, indicating the attentiveness and power of an Alpha? Or is your trunk bent forward, your head bowed, your shoulders drooped and chest sunken inward: indications of depression, dejection, and weakness? Did you know that such a posture inhibits breathing and can actually *increase* feelings of nervousness and anxiety?

Study your posture in a mirror—or better yet, in the videotape. An assertive stance—one in which you're standing erect, and leaning slightly forward—telegraphs confidence and self-assurance. Slouching, on the other hand, sends a submissive message. Do you orient your entire body towards someone when you speak to them, or merely turn your head? The latter signals reserve—and perhaps fear. People who lack confidence act like prey: they hunch their shoulders and lower their heads—or sometimes puff themselves up if they're trying to defend their space. An erect, relaxed body posture sends the message that you're at ease and confident—that this is *your* turf.

Remember to utilize what body linguists refer to as "antigravity signs": palms down, squared shoulders, lifted head and chin, and "standing tall."

A word about physical fitness, here. You need to appear as fit as possible. Physical appearance is the hallmark of the Alpha, because fitness makes three powerful subliminal statements: first, you are tough (you can fight); second, you have self-control (obesity suggests a self-indulgent nature which is ill-advised in a leader);

third, you appear sexually potent (a quality which virtually all species have been hard-wired to perceive as essential in a leader).

"Fitness" does not necessarily mean that you must look like a marathoner, a supermodel or a body builder. Lord knows, I certainly don't. But keep in mind that fitness can express itself subliminally through an individual's energy. If you move about a great deal, show real enthusiasm for your subject, and exude confidence, you will be perceived as fit. If you seem frozen to a spot, listless, and nervous, you're the classroom equivalent of a lame moose trapped in a snowdrift.

Micro-mini Digression: Teaching on Wheels

Several years ago, I worked with a wheelchair-bound professor who was concerned that her students seemed to view her as an object of pity — they tended to exhibit excessive politeness, wouldn't look her in the eye, and avoided meeting with her in her office. There was no real connection; if anything, there seemed to be real avoidance. She decided to try some of the Alpha strategies outlined in this book, and once she rolled out from behind her desk and began wheeling dervishly around her classroom, everyone relaxed. [12]

A year or so later, her long-awaited service dog (a gorgeous Golden Retriever) became available, and he was a tremendous advantage to this free-wheeling prof.

---

[12] She also began making outrageously funny comments about her disability: "Oh, I know what you're thinking. Such a lovely woman: why, it's terrible that she has that awful ... haircut."

I was not surprised. In the process of training service dogs, I have had to learn to maneuver wheelchairs in order to understand what skills my canine associates should have to best suit their handlers. I started out, of course, without the dog; I'm *way* too klutzy to handle two tasks at once. In my solo wheeling around the city, however, I discovered that people tended to avert their eyes as I rolled past. Well, of course. Americans have learned that it's "impolite to stare" when confronting the handicapped: I suddenly became invisible by simply sitting in a wheelchair. No one looked at me; no one spoke to me.

I had become an Un-person.

However, when I became adept enough to bring a dog into the equation (once I'd mastered the basics of wheelchair mechanics and started training my canine colleague), people suddenly began seeing me again—indeed, they even *approached* me to compliment me on my handsome, well-trained companion.

The presence of dogs in a classroom—any classroom—changes the atmosphere dramatically. Everything suddenly becomes more relaxed and friendly. A dog in the class of a handicapped professor, however, also eradicates the awkwardness and stress that inexperienced students suffer when encountering disability for the first time. Suddenly there's a furry facilitator who makes conversation easy.

But, back to the text...

Moving around is important. But even the most peripatetic of professors has to stand still *sometime*. And the manner in which you carry yourself gives important information to those around you—

especially to your students, who have gotten into the habit of watching your every move.

Body linguists frequently refer to posture as "closed" or "open." A closed posture tends to be a bit off-putting: leaning backwards, for example, usually signal aloofness—perhaps even rejection. Interested, open people tend to lean forward. Folding your arms across your chest or body can be seen as a defensive or protective gesture, and you'll seem closed, guarded and perhaps afraid.

Look in a full-length mirror. Sit down, fold your arms, cross your legs and turn your body away. Tilt your head down a bit. Do you look as if you're interested in what anyone has to say? Nope. You look hostile and defensive. Now stand up, plant both feet on the ground, tilt your head to the side, and show open hands. You look confident and accepting, right?

Now pretend you're a student. Which teacher would you prefer to have in class? Right. My point exactly.

9.4 Hands-on Teaching

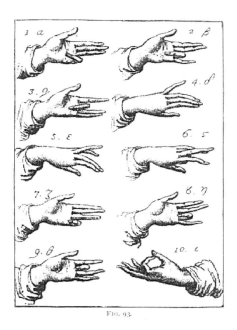

FIG. 93.

As long as you have the videotape player running anyway, make sure you pay careful attention to your gestures. They're extremely important: just think about the difference between a "palms down" and "palms up" gesture. The former signals control, the latter powerlessness.

Do you look as if someone has tied your hands behind your back—a passive stance if there ever was one? That's exactly how someone stands when s/he's lined up before the firing squad, for heaven's sake. Moving your hands and arms comfortably signals Alpha confidence and freedom. But don't overdo it. Too much gesturing can make you look silly or out of control, and may distract your students from what you're saying.

Hands are powerful tools for expression, but they can also be used to assert authority. Large, open gestures make you appear confident, open and honest. A pointed finger, or hands held closely together can emphasize not only what you are saying, but can once again take advantage of the students' prey drive. But there can be too much of a good thing. Making too many gestures—or the wrong gestures—makes you seem nervous—perhaps even out of control or laughable. And self-touching—wringing your hands, biting a nail, touching your face or clothing—usually indicates anxiety or nervousness.

Oh—and no matter how much that snagged nail or cuticle is driving you crazy, *never* raise your finger in class to chew on it—watch yourself do so in a mirror and you'll see why.

Looks terrible, doesn't it?

9.5 The Eyes Have It

T he eyes may or may not be a window to the soul, but they are definitely a good strategy for establishing yourself as a physical presence. Eye contact is essential to an Alpha. Border collies can control much larger animals—even a huge Brahma bull—by fixing them with a powerful stare, called, understandably enough, "eye" by their handlers. You probably don't want to go quite that far. A Death Stare tends to trigger flight response in most student and fight responses in Alphas (certainly if a student's eyes begin to widen as you look at her, glance away quickly). But you needn't glare; just make certain that you're looking directly into the eyes of your students (if you uncomfortable with this, look at their foreheads or noses. They won't be able to tell the difference.

Our eyes, after all, demonstrate where our attention is. Glancing at your watch while a student is speaking, for example, signals that you're more interested in the time than in what she's saying—*even if that is not the case.* Even something as apparently innocent as blinking can make a difference. The actor Michael Caine made a wonderful video called *Acting in Film* (1989, if you can find it, rent it), in which he demonstrated the difference between a blinking and unblinking gaze—the former made him look like a sheep, the latter like a lion. Try it in the mirror. Oh, and while you're there, remember that if you can't make a zygomatic smile—the kind that crinkles up the crow's feet around your eyes—don't bother. A polite smile indicates a lack of interest; a weak smile indicates fear; a fake smile can look like a snarl. Practice smiling with your eyes alone (your lips may twitch a bit). In fact, practice a full range of expressions, so that you can not only see what your class sees, but you can determine which are most effective.

Make direct eye contact whenever possible. Some women, particularly women from other cultures, have learned as children that it is more "feminine" to look away or look down. But remember that direct eye contact and a head held erect are essentials of Alpha behavior. You don't have to stare: just look the student directly in the eyes, then look at their mouth for a moment. Eye contact signals both control and respect: not only are you being assertive, but you're showing interest in and attention to what your student is saying. In addition, pay close attention to your facial expressions—use the videotape and a mirror. How do you express anger, joy, sadness, or fear? What do these expressions feel like in muscle memory? Practice making your face and head look assertive.

You can do it.

9.6 Space: the Final Frontier?

Okay. You now look and sound confident, and are ready to utilize one of the most strategic weapons in your Alpha arsenal—and one of which amazingly few teachers avail themselves: the classroom space itself. You can use that space to take absolute charge of a class with minimal effort and virtually no possible chance of failure: indeed, you have a decided edge here.

Try a single experiment and you'll see what I mean—even if you are the wimpiest, shyest, most anxious, nervous teacher to ever cower in front of a class. While your class is in progress, walk from the front of the classroom to one side or the other, and watch the entire dynamics of the room change. All of the students' heads will come up—they're watching you take control of your territory and they're fascinated. Watch the students who were slouched off at the side suddenly become aware that they are in the new "front" of the room when you stand next to them. They'll sit up straighter, perhaps start taking notes, and will be far more likely to answer a question you ask. Two things have caused this response: first, you've activated their prey drive, the hard-wired, centuries-old instinct to watch a moving object; second, you've made it clear that *the front of the room is where **you** say it is* simply by becoming a physical presence as opposed to hiding behind the lectern. You've marked your territory—and established that your territory is *the entire classroom space.*

After all, you can go wherever you like in the room, while the students must remain in their chairs. Indeed, students will generally raise their hands to ask permission to rise from their seats, even to go to the bathroom.

The power of space is an excellent reason, by the way, to avoid using the two most insidious articles of furniture in the classroom.

Mini-Digression

The Lectern and the Desk:
A Classroom Teacher's Two Worst Enemies

Ah, the perfidious lectern. It permits—actually even encourages—teachers to hide behind it, which effectively turns the professor into a human form of the tethered goat used as bait for the lion. You're *stuck* back there. Yes, it feels safe, but it sets up a virtual wall between you and your students. And it keeps you from your strongest classroom strategy: movement.

Even when teachers are assertive, the lectern can bring an air of confrontation to what would otherwise be a shared

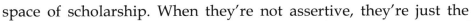

space of scholarship. When they're not assertive, they're just the academic version of prey. *Never stand behind a lectern unless you have no other choice whatsoever.*

Ditto the desk and chair in the front of the classroom. These two traditional pieces of pedagogical furnishings are perhaps even worse than the lectern. Same tethered-goat problem, but it's exacerbated by the fact that you are now on the students' level, trapped in your seat just as they are in theirs. You have given up your best opportunity for establishing your authority without confrontation: the classroom space itself.

End of Mini-Digression.
Meanwhile, back at the book...

D r. Edward T. Hall, a professor of anthropology at Northwestern University, coined the phrase "Proxemics" to describe his theories about personal zones and territory and how we use them. He posits that there are four distinct zones in which most people operate: public, social, personal, and intimate. We're all fairly comfortable in public space, watching a rock musician or presidential candidate from a distance, for example. And we'd probably be very pleased if the rock star or candidate entered our social space: "Wow! Mick Jagger/Senator X was sitting at a table only *this* far away!" If we *really* like them, we might even be willing to allow them into our personal or intimate space: "He came over, shook hands with me and then *hugged* me!"

But generally, we get very nervous when people move into that invisible three-dimensional "comfort" area surrounding us. That's why we sometimes feel uncomfortable when a stranger sitting next to us in an airplane or theatre hogs the armrest we share. Indeed, I've flown on very long flights where *neither* of us used the armrest.

Personal space can be a powerful tool in a classroom. Students having a whispered sidebar conversation? No need to scold and force a confrontation. No need to give them even so much as a dirty look. Just walk over near them—you're not making a statement; you walk around the class all the time now, remember?—and "accidentally" back into their space for just a moment, apparently unaware of what you've done. You won't be looking at them; your back (or side) will be turned toward them; you'll be addressing another student or the class as a whole (or listening to another student speak) at the time.

Now watch negative and positive reinforcement at work. The whisperers will stop. But best of all, they'll stop because your subliminal message makes them feel uncomfortable (negative reinforcement), and because as soon as they're quiet, you'll move away and the anxiety will cease (positive reinforcement).

They'll probably be completely unaware that you've carefully engineered the reinforcement, and thus you will have proven your control of the class — and them — in a friendly, non-threatening way: all the while smiling, talking, and making no reference whatsoever to their rude behavior.

You'll find that this non-confrontational maneuver works on virtually any sort of passive disruption whatsoever: even extensive navel-ring maintenance.

10
After the Camera Stops Rolling: Teaching With Alpha Rules

A s I noted earlier, if the class does get out of hand, it is probably a combination of lack of assertiveness on your part, plus a failure to watch your students carefully. You should be able to tell from their body language if they are insecure, uncomfortable, angry, or confused.

But, as we all know, control of a class is of course not *entirely* a manner of how you behave; it's how others behave as well. Even if you are clearly a super-Alpha, some high-level Alpha students may try to gain the upper hand (they're Alphas: it's their nature).

Much like Alpha dogs, Alpha students will try to push the envelope just as far as possible; even the most confident and assertive teacher will on occasion be backed into a corner by a classroom lawyer who has managed to find a loophole in the syllabus and will attempt to squeeze through it. Dealing with such situations is invariably uncomfortable: better to avoid them in the first place. Here's how.

You can control their behavior by making rules. Alpha students are, after all, rule-makers themselves: they understand how things work and tend to respect those who make rules and make them well. So here are a few basic Alpha rules that may prove helpful.

Before the semester begins:

A good deal of classroom disruption can be avoided long before class even begins. Even those of us who are not "natural" Alphas can still plan like ones. Here are some basic strategies:

1. Revamp your syllabus. Eliminate all possible loopholes that could conceivably lead to trouble—well, as many as are feasible. Of course, you won't catch them all—to do so would require a document roughly the size of the civil code. Put the syllabus on your web site and you can just keep adding section after section— an added benefit to doing so is that students who lose their copy will be able to download another rather than asking you for one. But keep in mind that the syllabus establishes you as the rule maker; it's important to Alpha students how well you make—and keep—the rules. The syllabus is essentially a contract between you and your Alphas (the other students use it only for information purposes). Make this contract as clear as possible; avoid all possible vagueness and ambiguity.

For example, I've found that it's a good idea not to accept "late" papers—unless the student also includes the hospital report and the license plate number of the bus that ran over him. How late is late? Specify a date *and time* by which all papers must be in your hands Otherwise, you'll find yourself in a debate over exactly what "due Friday" means. (I have been known to specify "Friday at 3:57 PM" as a due date in order to emphasize the fact that a "few minutes late" won't be acceptable; "Friday at 4PM" seems to be just a bit too hazy for many students). Explain that the US postal system and email are acceptable modes of submission, but that the sender uses them at her own risk: neither snow nor rain nor heat nor gloom of night, nor downed servers, will excuse a late completion of their appointed paper.

I balance my inflexible lateness policy with a very relaxed extension policy: if the student lets me know at least *seventy-two hours* before the due date that he'll need an extension, I'll generally grant it without question (an extension on a second paper is harder to get, on a third, almost impossible; I explain to students that this is because I don't want them getting overwhelmed by make-up assignments late in the semester).

Similarly (here's a practical example of negative aversion), I make it clear that make-up exams must be taken as soon as possible (generally within a week, unless there are serious documentable health problems involved) and that they will be significantly more difficult and time consuming than those taken with the regular class—the rationale here is that the student will have had more time to study. A standard poetry exam, for example, might be composed of ten author/title identifications and an essay chosen from five prompts; a make-up might be five essays using all five prompts. Not only does this keep the students honest, but there's a real benefit to me: I wind up escaping having to write a second exam, and giving *very* few make-up exams.

On the first day

1. **Get class acknowledgement (buy-in) of the syllabus**. Hand out the syllabus. Go over the syllabus in class. If the class is one with high levels of "natural" aversion (a required first-year composition or math class, for example), you might consider sending around two syllabi apiece: on for the student's use, and one for the student to sign and return to you to show that she has received the syllabus and accepted its rules. If it's a potential "problem" class, and if for some reason you find yourself needing to make changes in the syllabus during the semester, (if you've fallen behind in your schedule, for example), create and re-issue a new syllabus, and circulate a new signup sheet as well. Yes, this sounds obsessive and anal—and more than a bit defensive. But as I stated earlier, Alphas understand and respect rules—they're rule-makers themselves. And once they've accepted your rules, they'll abide by them.

2. **Synchronize your watches**. In the college where I teach, it seems as if every clock in the building is set to a different time. Your institution probably functions in the same manner. So, as Alpha, it's up to you to determine what time it is. Find a web site linking you to the WWVB Atomic Clock in Boulder, Colorado. Set your watch against it on a regular basis. Even better, buy a watch that automatically updates itself to the clock (Yes, I know that most such watches look clunky and nerdy; if it clashes with your power suit, just buckle the thing to the handle of your bookbag).

Explain to the class what you have done, and that all scheduling—class start times, class end times, and so forth—will be determined by the Boulder clock. It's their responsibility to be on time.

This way, everyone will know when the class starts (important in my classes because there's a quiz at the beginning of each class which, over the course of the semester, can have a significant impact on the final grade) when papers are precisely due (*e.g.*, by 3:57 PM on the assigned day—no exceptions), when midterms and finals begin and end, and when a scheduled appointment with me begins (important because I will wait no more than eight minutes for a student who fails to show up without notifying me that she'll be late: I chose eight minutes because it seemed a lot less vague than ten). And, perhaps even more importantly, they will recognize that you are not arbitrarily determining what is timely and what is late—they'll have to blame the Boulder clock for that.

3. **Control informality**—this is not to say that you cannot be informal, as long as students realize that *you* determine just *how* informal. Example: I let my students know during the first class that I prefer to be called "Darby." Should they feel uncomfortable without an honorific, I will allow them to use "Professor Lewes" (NEVER "Mrs. Lewes," which undercuts my position by not only obliterating my hard-earned doctorate but also making me sound like their moms). Allow food or beverages only in classrooms where you clearly have the upper hand. The Alpha controls who eats and when.

During the first week:

Schedule a short written exercise (worth minimal points) with a specific due date and time. Refuse to accept any late papers. Also schedule a required short (and preferably easy) quiz. If any students miss it, make them take a much harder make-up quiz. This allows students to realize early on that you're serious about such things without seriously jeopardizing their grade. When far more important papers and exams come up later in the semester, the rules will have already been made clear: no one will feel blindsided.

Throughout the semester:

1. Remember that **humor** is a form of non-confrontational confrontation which enables you to get your point across to your Alphas without having to take them on or embarrassing them in front of the pack.
2. Use body language to make or soften a point. Look students directly in the eyes—win *all* stare-down contests (if necessary).
3. Be able to shut an unruly Alpha down absolutely if necessary. (If all else fails, use the "bombshell" method outlined below at 10.4: immediately stop the class and release everyone except the troublemaker, then have a private talk.)
4. Be as clear as possible. Alphas hate to be confused—it makes them look helpless or dumb, and they'll feel they've suffered a loss of status, which they'll perceive as unfair punishment.
5. Try to work creativity into the assigned grade for any assignment. Alphas are generally highly creative and innovative, and enjoy such projects. In problematic classes (remedial or required first year), I let students turn in one-act plays, parodies, pseudo-interviews with historic figures, pseudo-psychiatric case studies, or comic strips in lieu of one of their essay assignments. If it makes a good point and makes for stimulating, enjoyable reading, they'll get an "A."
6. Use space control inside and outside the classroom. Arrive last in the classroom; make your students wait for you rather than vice versa. If a student is blocking your path in the hallway, wait for him to move out of your way—do not go around him. Subordinate animals move for the Alpha.

During finals and the grading period:

1. This is the only time when you can relax the rules with anything approaching impunity. Be more flexible with extensions (I'll generally require only twelve hours notice at this time) and make-up schedules. NOTE: Be careful here, however. It's extremely important to be consistent in enforcing all rules of the classroom. Rules are very important to Alphas; they'll get very exasperated — and sometimes downright angry — when rules are changed. Example: I used to give students extra days (at the last moment) when I knew that I would not be grading their papers right away. I assumed I was doing them all a favor, since most thanked me profusely. My Alphas, however, who had carefully planned on the original due dates (and had carefully worked their other classes' assignments around mine) were generally frustrated and annoyed. I learned to establish regular routines that students could depend on. Now, if I do extend a date, I try to do so at least two weeks in advance.

2. Try to schedule time with each of your students to go over their final grades in some detail. Very few students will argue about a grade if you've explained precisely why you're giving it, and they won't have the shock of receiving a lower grade than they expected in the mail (and having to explain it to their parents).

10.1 Non-confrontational Confrontation

onfrontation, like punishment, has no place in teaching.[13] It almost invariably leads to a direct escalation of hostilities rather than education. Be non-confrontational whenever possible. I cannot stress enough how important it is to work *with* your Alphas; to never challenge them directly unless you want your car covered with raw eggs and your teaching folder filled with terrible student evaluations. (If your Alphas hate you, so will everyone else in the class.)

Non-confrontation may sound like wimpiness or cowardice; it's not. Finessing a student requires far more craft and creativity than simply whomping them over the head with the power of your position—and finessing is far more successful when it comes to learning and growing. Students who have nothing/no one to fight against have no reason for hostility and are less likely to challenge authority. If the student says "$#%@" aloud when her "F" test is returned, for example, don't look shocked or scold her. To do so will be to offer up to the class a magic "Freak out the Teacher" button that they will push whenever they get bored.

Instead, use humor as a form of non-confrontational confrontation. Try saying something along the lines of, "Anne, please try to avoid the use of technical jargon." You've made your point; the class laughs; even *she* laughs. If a student tends to sleep in class (assuming that you've already made certain that he's not exhausted for a real reason, such as a full-time job on the side), show up with a can of cola and a chocolate bar and put them on his desk. Or have the entire class shout "wake up, John!" in unison. Or go over and

---

[13] At least not unless absolutely all else has failed, you're absolutely calm and in control, and you know absolutely what you're confronting and why. C'mon, now. How often does that happen?

stand next to his desk and kick the chair leg lightly. It's all done jokingly: no confrontation. John can laugh it off—and perhaps he'll begin retiring at a decent hour.

A Very-very Short Addendum:

Remember that humor extends to you as well. Gentle self-deprecating humor is a mark of self-confidence. Laugh at yourself when the opportunity arises: when I misspeak, for example, I shake my head and remark upon my "peech inspediment." Such humor can maintain classroom perspective and defuse confrontations. I've joked about my mid-life crisis motorcycle and sports car, my lack of high-level organizational skills, and the fact that I'm functionally innumerate.

Having no sense of humor about yourself will be perceived as a decided weakness—and a button that students will feel free to push whenever they're bored or unhappy.

Relaxing and not taking yourself too seriously will be seen as a decided strength.

10.2 The "Rent an Alpha" System

S ometimes classroom disruption is not really the students' fault. Frequently, students (particularly first-generation college students) simply *do not know how* to behave in class. They'll bring in food, or sleep, or read the newspaper, or carry on sidebar conversations, because that's how they behave at home.

I get around this problem with what I call the "Rent an Alpha" System. I usually have a student assistant every year, and she's invariably a well-known, well-respected, and well-liked member of the student community. If there's a class I'm worried about—let's say, a first-year composition class composed entirely of brand-new students—I'll employ my student worker as an in-class "teaching assistant." The students will have a great deal more respect for her opinions than they do for mine—she's their age, and obviously succeeding in college—and they'd like to do so too.

By modeling appropriate behaviors, she eliminates most confusion, confrontation, and hassle. If your college does not fund student assistants—or if you want to pack your class with more than one (a male and a female, for example)—the education department is a wonderful source of models. Even though they're not earning money, the opportunity to pad one's resume with "teaching assistant" experience for a few hours' work makes the position valuable. (Many—if not most—of my rented Alphas are heading for graduate school, and such experience may make the difference between winning or losing a valuable grad school Teaching Assistantship.)

10.3 The NFL Method

N o, not the National Football League. "NFL" here stands for "No Free Lunch." This does not mean no lunch at all—just that lunch (anything the students in a disruptive class want) must be earned. Students need not feel deprived—you might even offer them something extra (such as quarters, or an early dismissal) just so that they *can* be earned. A good example of NFL is the response paper I require of anyone who misses a class. They are allowed three "free" absences (missed classes that will not affect their final grade), but must still turn in a 1-2 page typewritten personal response to the assigned material for every absence—even the "free" ones. These responses are required, not optional.

My justification is that I want to make certain that students are not missing material that is bound to show up on the exam; thus they can't be angry with me, since I'm only attempting to protect their GPA. The reality is that students who might otherwise blow off class in order to sleep late will show up if only because they don't want to have to write the damned paper.

10.4 When All Else Fails: "Bombshell" Pedagogy.

This is an incredibly powerful tool, but it can be used—at most—only once a year, and only in the most extreme cases. Here's how it works.

Let's say you have an Alpha student who, despite your super-Alpha presence and careful attention to Alpha rules, constantly challenges you, disrupts the class, and seems to be actively looking for a fight. You've tried everything and failed. Here's what to do.

"Bombshell" Pedagogy

1. The next time she acts out in class, stand up and say, "Okay, that's enough. Everybody *out!*" (Slamming a book on a desktop gives extra emphasis). Then whirl and point to the disruptive student: "YOU stay." The student will stay—she knows that to leave would escalate things to Deanly levels, and anyway, she has been wanting a confrontation with you all semester, and you finally seem to have taken the bait.
2. Wait until everyone has left the room. The student will be quivering with adrenaline: here comes the battle she's been waiting for. You'll feel the electricity.
3. Sit down VERY close to the student: if possible, invade her personal space ever so slightly. Adrenaline levels will spark to even higher levels; the student may even lean forward in anticipation.
4. Then lean back slightly, turn your palms up, and say, "Jess, you are one of the best and brightest students I have ever encountered. There's no reason you shouldn't be acing this class and enjoying it. Clearly, I have let you down in some profound way. Help me, here. What can I possibly do to make this class work for you? I'm willing to try just about anything."
5. Student deflates. There's nothing to fight against; you've caved (although only after you demonstrated your ultimate power by releasing the class and keeping her behind).

I have used this method perhaps four or five times in twenty-odd years (some of them *very* odd) of teaching. Twice, the student apologized for the inappropriate behavior but pled circumstances where I was clearly at fault (unclear due dates for papers; unclear descriptions of upcoming tests). I apologized and immediately addressed the issues, creating a better classroom and making myself a better teacher in the process. The other times, the students came up with variations on a theme: "Aw, no; I was being a jerk; I'm having troubles (at home, at work, with my roommate, with money, with my girl/boyfriend); I'm really sorry."

The bottom line: If the student has nothing to fight against, she cannot fight. But there's no winner or loser. She hasn't been beaten; she's been *finessed*. When she leaves the classroom (and is confronted by a number of her classmates asking "What happened? What did she do to you?"), the student will be able to answer, *with no loss of face whatsoever*, "Oh, we worked things out. No big deal."

Everybody wins.

Boom.

11
Alphas in the Classroom

S/he who controls the Alpha dog controls the pack.
S/he who controls the Alpha student controls the
classroom.

A friend of mine in graduate school—I'll call her "Melissa"—was small, shy, and slender (she sometimes shopped for her dresses in the pre-teen section of the department store), and decided that having a large dog in her South Chicago apartment would make her feel safer. She found a sweet, neutered Labrador-German Shepherd mix at the pound, and brought him home.

She called him "Muffin."

Everything began well, but within a few weeks Melissa was feeling, well, a bit *too* safe. Muffin had taken charge of her life. True, burglars could not enter her apartment. But then, *no one* could enter her apartment—not repairmen, guests, or even her boyfriend—unless she first lured the dog into her study with pieces of chicken and then locked him in. He would then throw himself against the door, screaming and barking, until the guests left and he was released.

So much for quiet, relaxed dinner parties.

The only exception to the Muffin's "VISITORS DIE!" policy was a female classmate of Melissa's, also short and slender. She could visit at any time; for some reason the dog never growled or barked at her.

Really Extra-Short Digression

Here's an interesting story about this classmate, whom I'll call "Leah." She was another small, petite young woman — perhaps 5' and 90 pounds dripping wet. After studying very late at the library one night, she made her way home and took a short-cut through a poorly-lit park, where she was set upon by three thugs who intended to rape her. Unfortunately for them, they had no way of knowing that she had just gotten out of the Israeli Army three weeks earlier. Two wound up in the hospital with shattered kneecaps; the third, who had run off screaming into the night (you don't even want to *know* what she did to him), was later apprehended by the police when his co-thugs ratted on him. If dictionary editors ever decide to illustrate the definition of "Alpha" in the dictionary, I think they should feature a photo of Leah.

But Back to Melissa and the Dog ...

Muffin chose to sleep on the center of Melissa's bed — if she attempted to push him over to "his" side, he would growl at her. She would then curl up on the 17"-wide area of the queen-sized mattress he permitted her and try to sleep. Or retire to the couch.

She could not come within five feet of him while he was eating, or he would snarl at her. If he were playing with a toy, she could not take it away from him — you guessed it; he'd growl at her. Once, she was unable to go jogging because

> Be afraid. Be *very* afraid.

Muffin had taken possession of one of her running shoes and wouldn't give it back.

She was living in a canigarchy.

Eventually, when she could stand no more, she coaxed Muffin into her car with a quarter-pound of ground sirloin, and then drove him back to the pound. He was adopted by one of the kennel workers there, and, after a rigorous course of obedience training, miraculously reverted to his pre-Melissian gentle self and lived happily ever after.

Melissa was less fortunate. When she got out of grad school and began teaching, she found herself unable to control her classes. Students would openly hold sidebar conversations or pass notes during her lectures; in group work, they would never stay on topic for more than a few moments. They challenged her aggressively in class; if she lost her temper, they would laugh at her and mimic her high, whispery voice.[14]

In an attempt to punish the students, she toughened up her exams and grading policies; students complained to the Dean that she was "unreasonable and unfair," savaged her on class evaluations, and egged her car one evening when she'd worked late.

Hoping to assuage their anger, she brought home-made cookies to class, thinking that this would make the students "like" her. They liked the cookies, but their attitudes toward her remained at best contemptuous. She relaxed her exams and tried to bribe them with high grades—but that only resulted in fuller, ever harder to control classes.

---

[14] On Halloween, one student arrived costumed as Melissa: puffy sleeved Laura Ashley pastel dress, pony tail, Mary Jane shoes, etc.

She was not granted tenure, and eventually left the teaching profession.

I'm sure you can see the pattern, here. In the first case, her dog took over the Alpha position in her home, making it effectively *his* home. Every time she allowed the dog to growl at her and have his way, or attempted to placate him with food, she committed a wolfy faux paw. Things worked much the same way in the classroom.

Was she doomed to her fate?

After all, how could this petite, shy, whispery-voiced young woman, who couldn't even control her own *dog*, ever hope to control a bunch of high-spirited college students?

Well, there are ways. Many of which I've discussed above. But there's also one additional (and very sneaky) way to control a classroom.

After all, she didn't have to control all the dogs in the world. Just her own. And she didn't have to control the entire class.

Just the Alphas.

I do a great many "cold" teaching demonstrations at as part of my visiting workshop presentations. With no warm-up or introduction, I will be faced with a class of non-majors, many of whom have high levels of natural aversion to the subject I present: literature. Such a situation of course precludes any traditional "control" over the class—I don't know them, so we haven't had a chance to build up any sort of trust; I can't hold a grade over their heads. And yet the class moves smoothly, and things go well.

"You were really in control there," observers frequently tell me. "How did you manage to take over the class so quickly? That was really impressive."

Such a feat *would* have been impressive, if that's what I'd done.

But face it: I'm just not that good.

There's no way I'm capable of engaging—let alone "controlling"—a class of twenty-plus strangers who have been forced to show up and aren't in the least bit interested in what I have to say. Instead, I cheat—using the wolfy equivalent of smoke and mirrors.

I actually "control" only two or three students in the class: the Alphas. I first figure out who they are—and in a strange situation where most of the group is uncomfortable they're fairly easy to spot—and then make certain I keep them interested and focused. I let them show off a bit, made certain they aren't zoning out when I pay attention to the lower status class/pack members, all the while making sure that their exuberance doesn't get out of hand, and that they don't challenge me (I'll explain how below).

Melissa's nightmarish situation is an excellent example of a good—and selfish—reason to spend time and energy identifying your Alpha students. If your Alphas—the students that other students look to for leadership—have decided that the professor is worth listening to, the entire class will be attentive (that's why the "Rent an Alpha" method noted above works so well).

To the casual observer, the Alpha is just one of the students. But if a lower status student starts acting like a jerk, the Alpha will shut her down with a look or slight movement—no threats, no confrontation. The Alpha student is far more fluent in Generation Whateverspeak than I can ever hope to be, and thus far more effective at control than I am.

It works both ways, of course. If my Alpha students decide that my class is a waste of their time (if, like Melissa's dog and students, they don't even consider me a low-level Beta), then no amount of effort on my part will bring the rest of the class around. Forget threats, bribes, rewards, or promises. Paying attention to what I say will be viewed as geeky, uncool, Omega behavior.

By gaining the respect of and control over my Alpha dog, I control an entire pack. No Beta or Omega dogs in my home are going to get aggressive as long as they see their Alpha deferring to me. By gaining the respect of and control over my Alpha students, I control the classroom. The result is an easy, laid-back environment in which discipline seems to be a non-issue.

Once you are perceived as "cool"—*i.e.*, worthy of respect—by Alpha students, you will experience a positive classroom which will extend to highly positive student evaluations, and lead to high class enrollments, all without pandering or grade inflation. And, if your Alphas respect you, they will also be far more likely to accept—or at least try to accept—some of your more way-out ideas: if you clearly have reservations about racism, sexism, and homophobia, for example, even racist, sexist, and homophobic Alphas will tend to re-examine their own notions about such things. If you extend courtesy to Omega students, Alphas will try to do the same. If you are excited about your subject, Alpha students will try to find out why.

But, you might, ask, "exactly *how* do I gain and keep the respect of these Alphas without yielding control of my class room? These are *kids*, after all, emotionally and intellectually immature. They shouldn't be encouraged to *run* things. What I need is a text on *Zen and the Art of Alpha Maintenance*."

Okay.

12
Zen and the Art of Alpha Maintenance

Which of the following statements is correct, grasshopper?

An Alpha is a curse: s/he is always challenging, questioning, pushing the envelope, causing trouble.	An Alpha is a blessing: s/he is always challenging, questioning, pushing the envelope, causing trouble.

T he correct answer, of course, is "Yes." (You may applaud, but please use only one hand.)

Alphas are walking compendiums of opposition: the same qualities that make you want to strangle them make your life as a trainer or teacher worthwhile. The Alpha dog, for example, can be a total pain in the butt to have around. Often, it seems as if you can never really relax around her; she's always plotting: let her get away with one paw on the couch, and she'll go for two—next thing you know, she's up beside you, trying to cadge a tummy rub. Give her a five-minute tummy rub, and she'll try for ten minutes. She's relentless. Sometimes it seems as if the Alpha dog is never *quiet*, either physically or intellectually.

Yet the Alpha dog is a true partner and friend. She is fiercely loyal and will defend you with her life. She can withstand pressures and stresses that would reduce a lesser animal to quivering jelly. She will force you—if only by her expectations and abilities—to think faster and more efficiently than you thought you ever could. She is an eager, active learner who processes information as fast as you can provide it—indeed, by trying to keep up with her, you sometimes  wonder exactly who is the teacher and who the student.

Alpha students are exasperating and exhausting. They never seem to *settle*—either physically or intellectually. They are apparently incapable of accepting a fact as incontrovertible. They'll complain about the slightest ambiguity in an exam question—even if they got the question "right." If the Alpha is bored, you'll know it, and so will the remainder of the class, who will become bored in turn.

And if you ever once lose control of the class to the Alpha, there's a good chance that you'll never get it back.

Yet Alpha students are exciting and stimulating. They can energize a class by the sheer force of their charisma; they're usually born leaders. They're courageous, innovative thinkers, almost always willing to try out a new idea or method. They are constantly striving to find new ways of seeing things. If they respect you, they will generally see to it that everyone in the class behaves respectfully. If they enjoy the class, everyone will.

As I pointed out earlier, controlling one's Alphas is the quickest and most pleasant way to control an entire class. Clearly, Alpha care and maintenance is a component of effective teaching. Yet how can one attempt to manage such an unruly mass of opposing forces?

Through balance: a sort of pedagogical *feng shui*, in which you work with, rather than against, the Alpha nature. It's a matter of balancing the natural pack dichotomies of hierarchy / sociability and Alpha/omega in the classroom. Nothing is static; everything flows back and forth in a world in which two opposing ideas can exist simultaneously and harmoniously.

Well, at least simultaneously.

There's the matter of respect, for example: an essential component of Alpha maintenance. Most Alphas fully understand respect and all its permutations. They have a finely tuned sense of status that will extend to almost every aspect of your relationship.

Take papers, for example—when reading student papers, I used to have a tendency to do so with pen in hand, "correcting" "mistakes" as I went along, peppering margins with "AWK," "TENSE," "WC" and "SP" notations.

There were at least two problems with that sort of repair: first, it made me do all the grunt work, and second, it removed all the responsibility—and thus all self-respect—from the student. Beta/Delta/Omega students loved it. They could duly, dully, and perhaps even dubiously make the specific "corrections" I suggested, then resubmit the paper for the better grade I would have to give, since they had "fixed" everything. There was occasional resentment when the essay *still* didn't get the desired grade, but, being Betas/Deltas/Omegas, they smiled and saved up their anger for class evaluations.

Alpha students' papers, on the other hand, tended to resist my arbitrary corrections—there was a lot more intellect and creativity going on in them, and AWK or SP didn't really cut it. Alphas can get quite frustrated and angry (and rightfully so) if you seem to be bogged down in technicalities, and ignore their ideas.

So I tried something different—something which wound up benefiting not only my Alphas, but the rest of the class (and me) as well. Instead of mindless technical notations, I provided a short "review" of the paper, much like those provided by journal peer reviewers for articles submitted for consideration. I didn't deal with technical glitches (except in remedial classes, of course); if there were any, I explained that they should be taken care of in the writing center.[15]

My central focus was suggesting strategies for change rather than changes themselves (see examples of some of my student response papers in *Appendix 2*). I thus put all responsibility for revision (and re-vision) right where it belongs: squarely on the student. In doing so, I treat the student as a colleague rather than a rewriting robot — and give my emerging Alphas the respect they need in order to develop.

Or leadership. Of course, as the professor, you are the class leader: you choose the books, the syllabi; you write the examinations and determine final grades. You have the degrees, the certificates, the title—even the snazzy uniform (your academic robes). The Alpha knows that it is in her own best interest to show you appropriate respect. But remember that the Alpha is a leader as well, and one who is probably far more in touch with your class than you are — and more capable of taking them to uncharted heights or depths.

Remember that the Alpha student has a great deal of stress in a classroom setting–perhaps more than you do. You have found your place in your world, after all: you can function comfortably as a super-Alpha in your classroom, a co-Alpha at home or among your peers. When you go to conferences and meet superbly gifted people whose intellect dwarfs your own (happens to me *all* the time), you can even slip comfortably into a Beta or Gamma role, with a minimum of fuss and little or no loss of self-confidence.

The life of student Alphas, however, is not so secure or static. First-year Alphas often worry about proving their status in a foreign

---

[15] I use Barbara Walvoord's "Gateway Criteria" here pointing out to students that, like the "real world," I expect them to have mastered Edited Standard Written English (ESWE), and that *finished drafts* presented for a grade must have "no more than an average of two departures from ESWE per page" (Walvoord 77).

environment in an arena where competition is a lot fiercer than high school. Even more advanced Alphas must navigate a bewildering number of threatening situations every day. Think of it: how would you feel if every day you were forced to perform in front of your peers in a discipline that you believed made you look foolish? For me, hell must be a place where I spend eternity failing to work equations on the chalkboard while giggling devils make fun of me. Yet Alpha students, ever-mindful of the need to protect status, might face such situations on a regular basis during their undergraduate years.

Alphas are also various and complex. Some of them may be clichés, easy to spot: the star football player who may or may not feel ill at ease in a literature class; the brainy nerd who may or may not be socially maladroit; the socially adept class president who might work very hard, or might attempt to glide by on her not inconsiderable charm. More likely they'll be uneven blends of the three—or way-out neo-radicals existing on a plane you've never encountered before. They might feel ill-at-ease in your class because it threatens their status, or cocky because they consider it their turf, or bored because they consider classwork little more than an inconvenient interruption of their true interests. An Alpha might be a dynamic leader in his biology class, a disruptive troublemaker in German, and listless non-participant in English Lit—even if he's an English major.

How can one ever hope to "manage" such an unruly bunch? By borrowing strategies from nature—and here I will leave my human/canine model for a moment.

In the Olympic Games, the only events in which men and women compete as equals are the equestrian events. This is because human physical strength has very little to do with the outcome. The horses weigh between one and two thousand pounds, and the relative strength of a two hundred pound man or a hundred pound woman is negligible—neither can use sheer brute strength to dominate an animal of such size and power. If anything, a slightly-built woman has an advantage over a muscleman in, say, the show jumping ring: she isn't even tempted to fight her equine partner, while a muscular man, more used to solving problems by powering through them, might be. (Think judo, in which a slightly built man or woman can overcome a bulky attacker by using his superior weight *against* him.) What successful riders use instead is *finesse* and *balance* (remember the "bombshell" method above?).

Back to dogs: if I'm walking a Great Dane who wants to drag me down the street, I'm not about to engage in a pulling contest. I'm hardly what one would call slightly built, but I'm no Arnold Schwarzenegger. Even if I manage to hang on to the animal, my arms will ache for a week. So, instead of pulling, I'll get his attention by giving short hard pops on the lead that are too brief to pull against, and keep enough cookies in my pocket to make me more interesting than the wide world: I'll give the dog nothing to pull *against*, and a good reason not to pull. It won't be long before we come to terms: my terms.

Dealing with Alpha students involves a similar dynamic. Force and threats will just give them something to challenge.

Alpha-ness—both yours and that of your students—is more of an attitude than anything else, a matter of confidence and authority in the way you present yourself. Yes, it may seem much easier to demonstrate these qualities if you're a muscular six-foot male with a baritone voice, than if you're a hundred-pound five foot female soprano. But by realizing how Alpha assertiveness works, and working *with* rather than against it, you can wind up bringing out the Alpha not only in your students, but in yourself as well.

Conclusion

I have probably not told you much that you didn't already know; I've just put it in a different context. Some people are horrified by the notion of "treating students like animals." The fact, however, is that we are all animals, constantly bombarded by positive and negative reinforcement, constantly reinforcing our students, our colleagues, our spouses and our children, whether we mean to or not.

> " ...that is what learning is. You suddenly understand something you've understood all your life, but in a new way."
>
> — Doris Lessing

In education, however, an awareness of what we are doing is crucial: consider, for example, the powerful and devastating message you send when you casually glance at your watch when a student is speaking. Or when you respond to a student's line of reasoning with a vague "mhm" because you're already moving ahead to your next point.

You can use that powerful message well or badly. You can reinforce specific behaviors which will serve the student well, or you can punish students and turn them away from your discipline in particular and education in general. Punishment and education are antithetical, after all, for if the student has no control or confidence, then there can be no learning.

I deeply believe that despite the existence of yuppie pre-schools, prep-schools, colleges, and esteemed universities, all learning is fundamentally autodidactic: true understanding, true mastery of a subject takes place in the privacy of one's own head. The material cannot be handed to a student; she needs to actively make the attempt to reach out and grasp it and make it her own.

As I pointed out earlier, we cannot follow our students throughout life; we cannot even follow them through their four-year college experience. We must teach them to motivate themselves: we can do this by leveraging the basic elements that are hard-wired into the human (and canine) psyche: sociability, the play/prey drive exercised by "killing" a problem, and the competitive (especially the self-competitive) urge for higher status. Through behavior modification and the encouragement of self-motivation, we can truly bring out the Alpha potential of each and every student.

"The secret to happiness in life is to find something you'd pay to do and then find someone to pay you do it."

— Charles Edward Lewes, advice to daughter

Appendix 1
Poems

Porphyria's Lover

Robert Browning

The rain set early in tonight,
The sullen wind was soon awake,
It tore the elm-tops down for spite,
And did its worst to vex the lake:
I listened with heart fit to break.
When glided in Porphyria; straight
She shut the cold out and the storm,
And kneeled and made the cheerless grate
Blaze up, and all the cottage warm;
Which done, she rose, and from her form
Withdrew the dripping cloak and shawl,
And laid her soiled gloves by, untied
Her hat and let the damp hair fall,
And, last, she sat down by my side
And called me. When no voice replied,
She put my arm about her waist,
And made her smooth white shoulder bare,
And all her yellow hair displaced,
And, stooping, made my cheek lie there,
And spread, o'er all, her yellow hair,
Murmuring how she loved me—she
Too weak, for all her heart's endeavor,
To set its struggling passion free
From pride, and vainer ties dissever,
And give herself to me forever.
But passion sometimes would prevail,
Nor could tonight's gay feast restrain

A sudden thought of one so pale
For love of her, and all in vain:
So, she was come through wind and rain.
Be sure I looked up at her eyes
Happy and proud; at last I knew
Porphyria worshiped me: surprise
Made my heart swell, and still it grew
While I debated what to do.
That moment she was mine, mine, fair,
Perfectly pure and good: I found
A thing to do, and all her hair
In one long yellow string I wound
Three times her little throat around,
And strangled her. No pain felt she;
I am quite sure she felt no pain.
As a shut bud that holds a bee,
I warily oped her lids: again
Laughed the blue eyes without a stain.
And I untightened next the tress
About her neck; her cheek once more
Blushed bright beneath my burning kiss:
I propped her head up as before,
Only, this time my shoulder bore
Her head, which droops upon it still:
The smiling rosy little head,
So glad it has its utmost will,
That all it scorned at once is fled,
And I, its love, am gained instead!
Porphyria's love: she guessed not how
Her darling one wish would be heard.
And thus we sit together now,
And all night long we have not stirred,
And yet God has not said a word!

1836, 1842

My Last Duchess

Robert Browning

Ferrara, 15—

That's my last Duchess painted on the wall,
Looking as if she were alive. I call
That piece a wonder, now: Fra Pandolf's hands
Worked busily a day, and there she stands.
Will `t please you sit and look at her? I said
"Fra Pandolf" by design, for never read
Strangers like you that pictured countenance,
The depth and passion of its earnest glance,
But to myself they turned (since none puts by
The curtain I have drawn for you, but I)
And seemed as they would ask me, if they durst,
How such a glance came there; so, not the first
Are you to turn and ask thus. Sir, `twas not
Her husband's presence only, called that spot
Of joy into the Duchess' cheek: perhaps
Fra Pandolf chanced to say "Her mantle laps
Over my lady's wrist too much," or "Paint
Must never hope to reproduce the faint
Half-flush that dies along her throat": such stuff
Was courtesy, she thought, and cause enough
For calling up that spot of joy. She had
A heart—how shall I say?—too soon made glad,
Too easily impressed; she liked whate'er
She looked on, and her looks went everywhere.
Sir, `twas all one! My favor at her breast,
The dropping of the daylight in the West,
The bough of cherries some officious fool
Broke in the orchard for her, the white mule
She rode with round the terrace—all and each
Would draw from her alike the approving speech,
Or blush, at least. She thanked men—good! but thanked
Somehow—I know not how—as if she ranked
My gift of a nine-hundred-years-old name

With anybody's gift. Who'd stoop to blame
This sort of trifling? Even had you skill
In speech—which I have not—to make your will
Quite clear to such an one, and say, "Just this
Or that in you disgusts me; here you miss,
Or there exceed the mark"—and if she let
Herself be lessoned so, nor plainly set
Her wits to yours, forsooth, and made excuse
— E'en then would be some stooping; and I choose
Never to stoop. Oh sir, she smiled, no doubt,
Whene'er I passed her; but who passed without
Much the same smile? This grew; I gave commands;
Then all smiles stopped together. There she stands
As if alive. Will `t please you rise? We'll meet
The company below, then. I repeat,
The Count your master's known munificence
Is ample warrant that no just pretense
Of mine for dowry will be disallowed;
Though his fair daughter's self as I avowed
At starting, is my object. Nay, we'll go
Together down, sir. Notice Neptune, though,
Taming a sea horse, thought a rarity,
Which Claus of Innsbruck cast in bronze for me!

1842

Appendix 2
Student Response
Papers

Example 1: **English 221 (Survey) Thematically weak student paper on Jane Austen's** *Pride and Prejudice* **comparing three of the female characters in terms of the Romantic belle-ideal.**

Dear Jessica,

Here's my response to the intro and first chunk. Caveat: I'm going to be VERY picky here, but that's to your advantage; I'm trying to help you get the strong grade you deserve.

You're not really easing your readers into the paper—you're whomping us over the head with your thesis right from the get-go. Then you cover about six volumes of feminist theory in two sentences—making one HECK of a lot of assumptions and oversimplification. And there's also a problem with the tone. At best, inflated diction sounds pompous. At worst, it sounds silly. Don't work so hard at sounding "academic" and "important." Your in-class essays are witty and fun to read. Aim for that kind of tone.

You might also give the reader some background. Scout the library—or the Norton, if you must. Get a quote on the nature of the "belle-ideal." Try to avoid using the generalized term "women": are you talking about **all** women, here? Middle class women? Factory workers? Prostitutes? "The role of women" cuts across class boundaries and centuries, after all—you have to clarify which particular aspects will be under examination.

The first chunk has pretty much the same problems. You gallop into Jane Bennett as a "conventional ideal" without a word as to what those ideals were. True, you get around to them later, but the reader would feel a good deal less lost if you explained that female physical frailty and reserve—and, you might add—with all due respect to Jane—a certain intellectual (ahem) quietness—were seen as positive feminine attributes. Plus, weakness and reserve seem like an awfully short list of traits—surely you could come up with a few more? (Yes, there were far too many dashes in those last sentences. Sorry.)

Then there's your quotes and what you do with them. When you throw a long quote at a reader (and I see a VERY long one coming up in chunk two), you're asking one heck of a lot: the reader has to read through the thing, attempt to isolate the part that refers to what you're talking about, and then figure out precisely how the quote supports your assertion. Way too labor-intensive for a reader; all of that effort is *your* job. Don't use long citations; trim them down to essential words—all that stuff in there about Bingley has very little to do with the feminine ideal and nothing to do with the paragraph. In fact, it actually undermines your case, since Jane's reserve—which you present as a positive—might well have cost her a husband, were it not for the triple interferences of Fate, Lizzie, and Mr. Darcy. If you're going to set up Jane as the epitome of conventionality, why not talk about her credulousness—her willingness to believe the best of everyone in the face of overwhelming evidence to the contrary, for example (a trait that I suppose would be useful in a wife of the time).

I've also snuck a peek at your second chunk and I see a lot of the same problems—and in addition, there's way too much plot synopsis (remember, your assumed reader has already read *Pride and Prejudice*) and a bit too little explication of why the plot is important.

But don't panic. Here's what you need to do:

Find a quote—no longer than a short paragraph—which describes the perfect middle-class woman of the age. Middle-class is very important, since Austen doesn't really discuss the aristocracy or royalty, nor does she seem particularly interested in the plight of the working woman. You can use the quote as an epigraph, or work it into the opening paragraph (hint: if you do use it as an epigraph, try to find one that's interesting or outrageous enough to catch and hold readerly attention)

Identify the three aspects of ideal womanhood you'll be examining. The quotes you've chosen suggest physical and mental—qualities: emotional qualities could make up the third.

Try to lighten the tone of the intro. Use Austen as a model for your prose style (you could do a lot worse).

Write a short intro paragraph for the Jane section, explaining how Jane typifies conventionality. Follow this with three paragraphs using the physical/intellectual/emotional paradigm. Use a strong topic sentence for each section. Use short quotes that demonstrate your point exactly; cut any extraneous verbiage. Make certain each section has the essential components of a critical paragraph: your point, textual evidence to prove that point, and argument, in which you explain precisely how the textual evidence proves

Do this with Lydia and Lizzie as well.

Make your points clear. Don't expect the reader to do any work except reading and following your argument.

Write a conclusion that restates your thesis. Keep it light.

Go back and make sure that every word you use means what you think it does. I had problems with your use of "resonates" to describe Jane's passivity, for example ("Jane's passivity resonates throughout the book").

YOU WILL BE FINE. Just try to relax and enjoy this essay. Talk to me if you want to discuss this further.

Darby

Example 2: English 314 (Romantic Literature) Structurally weak student comparison of Shelley's "Alastor" and Byron's "Manfred."

Dear Stephen,

This is a lot more focused. Now we have something to work with. So here goes…

Some technical problems: parallel construction (if it's Shelley's Alastor, then it has to be Byron's Manfred as well), some awkward diction ("written at the same time" sounds almost as if Byron and Shelley were in the same room, madly racing one another to finish their respective works), poor word choice (look up the meaning of "escapade" and you'll see it doesn't really fit the dark tone of these poems), organization (if Shelley comes first in the initial sentence, he'd darned well better come first in the entire paper), and some fairly goofy parentheticals which seem rather like a footnote-type commentary, ("Byronic hero") yet which require a whole lot of effort on the reader's part. You need to at least explain what a Byronic hero *is*. Remember—you're not writing for me, but for your peers.

Good points include an excellent grabber, a first-rate proto-thesis (although "Perhaps" is really a wishy-washy way to begin a thesis statement), and a map of sorts. The map needs tinkering with: you must straighten out the awkward diction. Also—what do you mean by "common woman"? A woman of the streets? A lower-class woman? Or, if I'm applying the term as I think you intended it, a very "uncommon" woman indeed: an ethereal spirit.

I'm also unsure about the function your second paragraph serves. It sounds sort of like a second intro. At first I thought that it was the intro to your first chunk—which would have been fine—but since it only discusses Alastor, that cannot be. If you want to use it as the chunk intro, discuss the ideas that you'll be proving in the chunk: here, according to your map, we should be reading about "the female [who] is not common." But you've gone off on a series of tangents that have little or nothing to do with common or uncommon females.

Technical and organizational glitches are going to wreak havoc with your grade, and the paper is peppered with them.

Okay. Step one. NEVER sacrifice clarity for style. I not looking for important, "academic" sounding prose; I want a clear thesis and a lucid argument. Good heavens; you're incredibly articulate in class, and would never in a million years blurt out something along the lines of "affords to their modifications a variety not to be exhausted." What is "non-society"? Why are you suddenly penning overwrought statements such as "these objects cease to suffice"?

Step two. Straighten out your organization by making sure you have the following:

INTRO
a "grabber" (you're in good shape here)
An absolutely clear thesis sentence which could not be mistaken for anything else. (ditto)
A clear, technically perfect "map" of the essay, which will keep both you and your reader on track.

FIRST CHUNK

A clear statement indicating what issues will be examined in this section (usually, the first point offered in the map.
A section which examines how Byron (or Shelley, if he's going first) deals with the topic

A section examining how Shelley deals with the topic
A section explaining the differences between the two works *and why they are important.*

CHUNK TWO AND THREE — same thing

This sounds like a LOT of work, but overall, you can save almost everything you've put into the paper if you'll just straighten out the diction and organization and throw in some **very** strong topic sentences. I'd like to see the new, improved intro tomorrow if possible,

Don't panic. You can do this.

Darby

Example 3. English 315 (Victorian Literature) Stylistically weak (and excruciatingly dull) student paper on *Jane Eyre*.

Dear Kirby,

Here's my response to your intro and chunk.

First, there's the question of tone. Face it; your thesis that Jane is a "control freak" is delightfully outrageous, and you need to have a bit more fun with it. Try easing up and dumping some of the "academic" diction, which is a tad inflated. You're using words that really do not mean what I think you intended them to (check out the dictionary for the meaning of "soujournment"): surely Jane is more than "distressed" in the nightmarish red room? How about flat-out terrified?

The writing center will be a help with problems of diction and tone—but I think you need to relax into this paper a bit (more on this below).

Now for the paper itself. The intro is not particularly effective—you make the same point again and again, not really developing it, just repeating it. Arguing that Jane is "similar" to a control freak doesn't really work, since you're arguing that Jane Eyre actually exemplifies such a type. The fact that she takes control "many times" doesn't help your thesis much—after all, you're going to be arguing that Jane takes charge **every** time—although it may take a gap of several months or years for her power to be revealed (she seems to leave Gateshead as a victim, but her return shows that she was indeed in control; similarly, her flight from Thornfield, while apparently the panicky escape of a powerless, penniless, friendless soul, is later seen as the temporary removal of the true head of the house).

Another major problem is that you tend to focus on plot rather than on your thesis. As I said in class, you are to assume that your reader has already read *Jane Eyre*. And right now, you're doing little more than **listing** examples of Jane's need to control. That gets stale rather quickly.

Frankly, at this point I'd pull back and do some (VERY minimal) research. You might, for example, draw upon your psych minor and ask one of your profs where you could find a clinical description of a control freak (or whatever the scientific term is to describe one). Then you could show how Jane—in each of her incarnations—exemplifies that type of personality. It would help if you could show why control freaks are the way they are (which I believe has something to do with a powerful figure dominating them in their formative years) and show how Jane's background follows the pattern.

Remember how we joked about a pseudo-case study of Jane as psychiatric patient? Why not try it? Think about how much fun you'd have writing from the point of view of a psychiatrist who was analyzing her. You could write up the entire paper as a one-act play. You've read myriad psychiatric case studies for your major, and have a feel for the language and the format; you could parody it. This could be FUN!! Right now, though, even you have commented that the essay is frankly boring, and the language feels labored and uncomfortable. You're clearly not enjoying writing this paper. Which usually means that I'm not going to enjoy reading it. And I've got the red pen with your grade in it.

Throw off all notions of a "term paper" for now. More importantly, don't worry about the grade for now—trust my ability to read intelligently and your own originality and creativity. C'mon— you're bright, articulate, and you have a wonderfully wicked sense of humor when you want to. Relax a little, and you could make this piece wonderful to read.

See me if you want to discuss this, or call me at home. Remember: have fun!

Darby

Index

Selected Bibliography

Benjamin, Carol Lea. *Mother Knows Best: The Natural Way to Train Your Dog.* Howell, 1985.

Cohen, David. "Behaviorism," in *The Oxford Companion to the Mind,* ed. Richard L. Gregory. Oxford, 1987, 71.

Cooper, Pamela J., and Kathleen M. Galvin. *The Basics of Speech; Learning to Be a Competent Communicator.* McGraw-Hill / Contemporary, 2001.

Dreikurs, Rudolf *et. Al. Logical Consequences: A Handbook Of Discipline.* Meredith, 1968.

Friedan, Betty. *The Second Stage.* Summit, 1986.

Hall, Edward T. *The Silent Language.* Doubleday, 1959.

Johnson, David W., Roger T. Johnson, Karl A. Smith. *Cooperative Learning: Increasing College Faculty Instructional Productivity.* Wiley, 1992.

Kohn, Alfie. *Punished By Rewards: The Trouble with Gold Stars, Incentive Plans, A's, Praise, and Other Bribes.* Houghton Mifflin, 1999.

Lewis, Janet R. *Smart Trainers; Brilliant Dogs.* Canine Sports Productions, 1997.

Plato. *The Republic.* Trans. Allan Bloom. Basic, 1991.

Pryor, Karen. *Don't Shoot the Dog! The New Art of Teaching and Training.* Bantam, 1999.

Skinner, B.F. *Beyond Freedom and Dignity.* Hackett, 2002.

Walvoord, Barbara, Virginia Johnson Anderson, Thomas A. Angelo. *Effective Grading: A Tool for Learning and Assessment.* Jossey-Bass, 1998.

> "When we judge a man not by his car but by his conversation, not by his house but by his books, we may have a land fit for teachers to live in. "
>
> —Hilda Neatby

"The average Ph.D. thesis is nothing but a transference of bones from one graveyard to another."
J. Frank Dobie

"Academy: A modern school where football is taught."
- Ambrose Bierce, *The Devil's Dictionary*

"Those who can do.
Those who can't teach.
Those who can't teach train teachers.
Those who can't train teachers write teacher training textbooks.
Those who can't write teacher training textbooks write state assessment tests."
—Steve Nordby

"Somebody has to do something, and it's just incredibly pathetic that it has to be us."
—Jerry Garcia